Dedicated to my Papa Charles

Dear Reader,

I decided to write this book because I thought it would be something that my grandfather would enjoy reading. My main goal was to tell the story of each artist featured on the Country Music Highway ranging from their childhood to their musical success. Additionally, I wanted to tell the history of the highway and give information about the artists' hometowns since I'm sure it helped shape their childhood and the adults they became. I included a section featuring other Kentucky artists who are notable but aren't on the "highway."

I spoke with family members and friends of the various artists so that I could learn details that weren't widely published. I appreciate them taking the time to speak with me and sharing their memories; they were both interesting and helped to make the book more complete.

My Mom and I met with Kebo Cyrus, brother of Billy Ray Cyrus. Kebo, a musician himself, was very friendly and open. In addition to showing us his and Billy's childhood home, where we got to look at family photos and meet his pets, he told us stories about the two of them growing up. Kebo also discussed his own musical experiences, let us listen to his latest CD, and gave us an autographed copy.

Shannon Stewart, daughter of Gary Stewart, and I talked on the phone. She was friendly, spoke highly of her father, and was anxious to talk about his accomplishments. Shannon described her father as someone who was always willing to help someone and that he was unique that way. My first thought was that Gary sounded "very Kentucky" since I know many Kentuckians who are very willing to help those in need. Shannon said that she wanted "everyone in Kentucky to know how much I love Kentucky and everyone there was just so great when I came to visit." She also expressed an interest in visiting the state again soon.

I received a nice letter from Mike Lewis discussing his friendship with Gary Stewart and his family. Mike recalled how he and Gary would sometimes trade guitars and described the experience of watching Gary play his Les Paul at a show as "one of the proudest moments of my life." We followed up the letter with a friendly and interesting phone discussion where Mike further described his relationship with the Stewart family.

My husband and I visited the David A. Zeeger Coal-Railroad Museum in Jenkins, Kentucky (Gary Stewart's hometown) and met Lois Greer, the museum's curator, and Lorena Hill. Both of these ladies were very friendly and forthcoming with sharing information about Gary returning home to play a concert in Jenkins. According to both of them, the concert was a huge success and the whole town was excited to have him home.

Lorena suggested I speak with Ernestine Flint who organized the Jenkins Homecoming Days Festival the year that Gary Stewart played. She was pleasant to speak with and shared details about the concert.

My husband and I met with Ricky Skaggs' brother, Garold Skaggs, and his wife, Janie. They were both pleasant, friendly, and willing to share information about Ricky, his childhood, and their family. Garold spoke highly of his parents, Hobert and Dorothy, and discussed how someday he would like to write a book with the main focus being on them and their lives. Janie's family grew up near the Skaggs family and her brother, Dickie, would play music with them.

I spoke with Tim Brown, son of Hylo Brown, on more than one occasion and found him to be good-natured and proud of his father's accomplishments. He recalled how his father got his start in music and his induction into the Grand Ole Opry. Tim, who is currently working on a book about his father's life, was kind enough to share photos of his father.

Tommy Boyd, a member of Dry Branch Fire Squad, and I exchanged several emails. Tommy discussed what it was like to work with Hylo Brown and Ricky Skaggs. His emails were both polite and informative. I particularly enjoyed a story he shared about his father-in-law, Ernest Preston, and Hylo being childhood friends.

Bill Purk and I exchanged emails about his friendship with Hylo Brown. He had helped to organize a concert to honor Hylo. Bill was helpful and described Hylo as "humble and kind." Through Bill, I spoke with Floyd Alexander whom had no idea that I would be calling but was both pleasant and polite. He discussed his experiences as a musician and described what it was like to work with Hylo.

I spoke with Keith Whitley's brother, Dwight Whitley, and his wife, Flo, on a couple of different occasions. I found them both to be cordial and helpful in providing information about Keith and his musical experiences. Dwight remembers all of the guitars that Keith owned and recalled recognizing country artist Chris Young playing one of them while he and Flo were watching the *Grand Ole Opry*. Before singing Keith's song "Don't Close Your Eyes," Chris explained that his guitar had belonged to the "late, great Keith Whitley" and that it was his first time playing it.

I spoke with Tommy Webb, of the Tommy Webb Band, about how he got his start in music and his experiences with his band. He was friendly and, in addition to answering my questions, sent me information on his band, a CD, and an autographed photo. I've had the opportunity to see the Tommy Webb Band in concert twice and enjoyed the show both times.

I spoke with Jim Burchett, of the Tommy Webb Band, about his experiences with the band and his childhood friendship with Keith Whitley and Ricky Skaggs. Jim was pleasant and explained how when he performs at a show he's interested in the audience having a good time.

I exchanged emails with Marlow Tackett's daughter, Racheal Friend. She was forthcoming and proud of her father.

I also wish to thank my parents, Cliff and Judy, my husband, Steve, and my brother, Damien, for traveling with me to the artist's hometowns, their input and "editing skills," and for their love and support.

Tiffany

The Country Music Highway is a 144 mile stretch of U.S. 23 that runs north to south across Eastern Kentucky. The highway crosses seven counties and represents the unusually high number of country musicians from the region. The "renaming" was the result of a bill sponsored by Representative Hubert Collins that passed through the Kentucky legislature on March 1, 1994. Due to the work of Congressman Hal Rogers, the Country Music Highway was added as a National Scenic Byway in June 2002.

Eastern Kentucky is located to the west of the Appalachian Mountains. Due to this proximity to the mountains, much of the area's economy has been coal based for a number of years. Many of the towns and communities were started by the coal companies so that workers could live close to the mines. Today, the landscape of Kentucky's economy has changed and, as a result, there are not as many coal and coal-related jobs as there once was. Although the number has declined in recent years, coal trucks still travel Kentucky's section of U.S. 23 on a regular basis.

Eastern Kentucky has a rich history of Appalachian music including bluegrass and country. This music has united families and neighbors and has been passed down for generations. Today, Appalachian music is still celebrated and enjoyed in many communities throughout Eastern Kentucky.

Lloyd, Kentucky

Lloyd, Kentucky is a small unincorporated farming community in Greenup County. It is located along the river and is the home of Greenup County High School.

Jason Carter

Jason Carter was born February 1, 1973 in Ashland, Kentucky to his parents Bruce and Sue Carter. He was raised in Lloyd, Kentucky along with his brother, Jeff, and was surrounded by pickers and singers. At eight years old, Jason's father taught him to play guitar. He later learned to play mandolin and spent most of his free time playing music.

Jason had the opportunity to play alongside his father in the James River Band which exposed him to local styles. In high school, Jason's father and uncle took him to several bluegrass festivals which allowed him to play with outside musicians during jam sessions. These musicians included Ralph Stanley, Dave Evans, and Doyle Lawson.

Jason was at a bluegrass festival the first time he saw Del McCoury perform. At age sixteen, he set his sights on playing with McCoury but decided he needed to learn the fiddle since the band already had a guitarist and mandolinist. It took him two years of practice to reach the standard that would be required for him to join McCoury's band.

In 1991, after graduating from Greenup County High School, Jason moved to Nashville, Tennessee where he landed his first professional job as a fiddle player with The Goins Brothers. The band traveled mostly throughout the East Coast.

In 1992, The Goins Brothers performed a show in Nashville with McCoury. Jason asked McCoury for a job and was given an audition two weeks later. He performed shows with the band in Nashville, West Memphis, Tennessee, and Garland, Texas. After returning home, McCoury hired Jason to play fiddle and sing baritone with the band.

Jason released his solo album <u>On The Move</u> in 1997. The album featured a number of songs including "Pretty Little Indian," Bill Monroe's "Methodist Preacher," "Chicken Under the Washtub," and his self-penned "Carter Country."

Jason also performs with The Travelin' McCourys, a band featuring McCoury's two sons, Ronnie on mandolin and Rob on banjo. The ensemble is rounded out with Jason playing fiddle and Alan Bartram on bass. In 2016, he paired up with fellow Kentuckian Michael Cleveland on the track "Tall Timber," with appeared on Michael's album <u>Fiddler's Dream</u>.

Jason won the IBMA Award for Fiddle Player of the Year in 1997, 1998, 2003, 2013, and 2014. In 2015, Jason's name was added to the Country Music Highway. At the event, he remarked, "This is such a great honor. So many wonderful musicians come from this part of the country. I grew up just about one block from here, and having my own community to offer their support like this is just an amazing thing." He added, "I'm just kind of blown away by it. I can't think of anything I could be more proud of than to be recognized in my hometown and my home state."

Jason lives in Cottontown, Tennessee with his wife, Heather. In his spare time, he enjoys sports of any kind, golfing, fishing, and gardening.

Flatwoods, Kentucky

Flatwoods, Kentucky is the largest city within Greenup County and has a population of 7,423 according to the 2010 census. This area of Eastern Kentucky was originally named Advance due to the fact that Advance United Methodist Church formed a Sunday school there in 1860. It was later changed to Cheap after John Cheap, who was a blind clergyman.

When the post office was formed in 1918, the name of the city reverted back to Advance. In 1938, the name of the post office was changed to Flatwoods and the city was incorporated using the same name. The name was chosen due to the fact that the area's topography is unique compared to most of Eastern Kentucky. The city consists of totally flat to rolling land that sits on a single elevated hill.

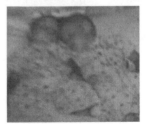
Billy and Kebo

Billy Ray Cyrus

Billy Ray Cyrus was born William Ray Cyrus on August 25, 1961 to Ron Cyrus and Ruth Ann Adkins. Billy was raised in Flatwoods, Kentucky along with his two brothers, Kevin (better known as Kebo) and Mick, and three sisters, Angie, Lisa, and Cherie. His parents divorced when he was five years old. Billy lived with his mother and stepfather, Cletis, while his father and stepmother, Joan, lived less than a mile away.

Billy grew up in a musical family. In an interview with Glenn Beck for CNN, he described part of his childhood, "Well, my earliest memories are Saturday nights at my Papaw Casto's house. Papaw means grandfather. And so I'd be at my Papaw Casto's house, and my mom would play the piano and my Papaw Casto would play fiddle. And my uncle and dad played the guitars, and we'd sing bluegrass, like, "Won't You Come Home, Bill Bailey" and "Roll in My Sweet Baby's Arms"."

Billy's Grandpa Cyrus was a Pentecostal preacher and on Sunday mornings the family attended his church. In the Beck interview, he described this and how his father was part of a gospel quartet, "[On] Sunday mornings, we'd be in his church where he would preach. And he would preach. And my Dad had a gospel quartet called the Crownsmen Quartet. And they were very successful in the Kentucky, Ohio, West Virginia realm there, you know, kind of like the same circuit where my Papaw would go to these revivals and stuff."

He continued, "And my dad would do these singings and up these hollers and stuff. And I'd go with him, and you know, we'd sing "Swing Down, Sweet Chariot," "Old Rugged Cross," and "I'll Fly Away." And it was feel-good music, both the bluegrass and the gospel, southern gospel. It was all feel-good music. And to this very day, that's what I like to do, is make music that moves people." Kebo, who would also sometimes travel with the quartet, hopes Billy and him can record an album featuring The Crownsmen's songs entitled <u>Sons of the Crownsmen</u>.

Billy attended Russell Independent Schools and lived less than a block from McDowell Elementary School. As a kid, Billy and Kebo enjoyed climbing trees, playing hide-n-seek after dark, building dams in the creek, and squirting each other with the water hose. Billy and Kebo, who played guitar, would perform George Jones songs in the family room with Billy using a broomstick as a microphone.

While attending Russell High School (Russell, Kentucky), Billy, a natural athlete, played both baseball and football. After graduating in 1979, Billy attended Georgetown College (Georgetown, Kentucky) on a baseball scholarship and dreamed of playing for the Cincinnati Reds like Johnny Bench.

When Billy was eighteen or nineteen years old, he says that he started hearing a voice repeatedly telling him to buy a guitar and start a band. During the Beck interview, he described the voice and his experience at a Neil Diamond concert, "I kept hearing this voice saying, 'This is your purpose in life. Your purpose in life is to make music. You need to buy a guitar.' And I'm going, why, why, why?"

He continued, "When I went to this concert, I heard Neil Diamond saying, 'You know what? It doesn't matter if you're white or black or rich or poor or a man or a woman. If you believe in your dreams and have faith, you know, you can do anything in this world that you believe you can do.' Right then it's like I had hands on me, saying, that's your purpose. I bought a guitar the next day, and that voice said, buy a left-handed guitar."

Billy had been left-handed and footed his whole life but didn't know that there was a difference in guitars. When he was young, he would pick up his dad's guitar and try to sound like everyone else but just couldn't play. After buying the left-handed guitar, he realized it was because he had it upside down.

In 1982, Billy and Kebo formed the rock band Sly Dog named after their one-eyed dog. The brothers, along with the other band members, began rehearsing in their childhood home. Billy was working in construction and trying to find the band venues to play. This proved to be a difficult task so Billy set a self-imposed deadline of ten months to find steady employment as a musician. In the meantime, Sly Dog played various places including parties, a show at Summit Elementary (Summit, Kentucky), and a performance at Greenbo Lake State Park (Greenup, Kentucky). One week before the deadline, Sly Dog was hired at Changes, a bar in Ironton, Ohio.

Sly Dog, primarily a rock-n-roll cover band in the beginning, performed songs by artists such as Bob Seger, Lynyrd Skynyrd, and Credence Clearwater Revival. The band played four sets a night, five nights a week, and began to develop a loyal fan base. During these performances, Billy would sometimes dance during guitar solos or hoist Kebo up onto his shoulders.

Billy was traveling to Nashville, Tennessee almost every week to play his latest song in an attempt to get a record deal. However, he wasn't having any luck as most people wouldn't talk to him and those that did told him he was too rock 'n' roll.

In 1984, there was a fire at Changes that destroyed the building and all of the band's equipment. Prior to the fire, Billy had found a Bible on the bar floor that he had stored in the back of his guitar amplifier. While surveying the damage, Billy saw something white inside his amplifier that was melted like a candle. Using a flashlight, he found the Bible parted and read the phrase, 'With every adversity lies the seed to something better.' According to Billy, he felt hands on him saying since Nashville says you're too rock 'n' roll then you're supposed to go to Los Angeles.

A few days later, Billy moved to Los Angeles, California and began looking for a record deal. However, he was continually told that he was to country for rock 'n' roll. To support himself, he worked as a car salesman. Eventually, Billy decided it was time to come home so, in 1986, Kebo drove to Los Angeles and picked him up.

Once back home in Kentucky, Billy joined Kebo's band, Main Street, and started playing at the reopened Changes. The band changed its name to Billy Ray and the Breeze, after a favorite Lynyrd Skynyrd song. Billy resumed his weekly trips to Nashville in search of a record deal. Later the same year, Billy met Cindy Smith and the two quickly eloped. Shortly after, Billy Ray and the Breeze fell apart so Billy joined the band The Players. In 1988, the band started playing four nights a week at the Ragtime Lounge in Huntington, West Virginia.

In July, Billy signed with personal manager Jack Madden. In hopes of getting Billy a record deal, Madden convinced Harold Shedd, of Mercury Records, to send Paul Lucks, also with Mercury Records, to one of Billy's shows. Lucks was impressed after watching Billy open up for Reba McEntire in Louisville, Kentucky. Shedd, still unsure, sent Buddy Cannon, a label representative, to see Billy perform at the Ragtime Lounge. Cannon reported that he hadn't witnessed a similar scene since Elvis Presley.

Shedd and Cannon both suspected that the major excitement of the crowd had been a setup for Cannon's benefit. As a result, the pair decided to travel unannounced to the Ragtime where they witnessed a very similar scene. Ultimately though, Shedd decided Billy might not be accepted as a true country artist so he passed on signing him.

Still determined to get a record deal, Billy managed to get a five minute meeting with Shedd in 1990. Billy played the song "Some

Gave All" which he had written about a Vietnam veteran in 1989. After listening to the song, Shedd stood up and said he was going to structure Billy a 'little deal.' He left and came back with the head of the label who shook Billy's hand and said 'Welcome to Mercury Polygram Records.'

Around this time, the name of the band was changed to the previously used Sly Dog. Billy began recording at Music Mill Studios and wanted to use Sly Dog as his backing band. It was a struggle but he eventually convinced the Music Mill sound producers to give the band a chance. The band demonstrated their talent and, as a result, were included in the official recording sessions.

While recording his album, Billy listened to a rough work tape of the demo "Don't Tell My Heart." He loved the song so he worked it up with his band and began playing it in concert. Immediately, people started requesting the "Achy Breaky" song. Billy felt that the title was wrong so he convinced the record company to change it to "Achy Breaky Heart."

On January 3, 1991, Billy officially signed his recording contract with Mercury Records at the Paramount Arts Center in Ashland, Kentucky. He was joined, at the press conference, by his parents, Mercury Record associates, local media, and about 300 fans. Later that year, Billy and Cindy amicably divorced. Cindy has songwriting credits on two songs, "Wher'm I Gonna Live" and "Some Gave All," that are included on Billy's first album, <u>Some Gave All</u>.

During discussions of how to promote Billy, the idea of creating a special dance for one of his songs was agreed upon. Melanie Greenwood, using inspiration from Billy's own dance moves, created the Achy Breaky dance. In January 1992, Greenwood and three dozen dancers filmed an instructional video for the Achy Breaky at the Holiday Inn's Red Fox Lounge in South Point, Ohio.

For his first video, Billy had hoped to convince Mercury that, in order to show his roots, the video should be filmed at his childhood home. He wanted to include shots of his mother sitting at her piano, her working in the kitchen, and of the handmade wire cage where his pet raccoon, Rascal, lived. Mercury didn't take Billy's suggestion but, as a compromise, agreed to shoot the video at a location near his hometown.

On January 21 and 22, the video for "Achy Breaky Heart" was filmed at the Paramount Arts Center. The first day of shooting mainly focused on getting shots of Billy and Sly Dog. Approximately 1,100 people attended the second day of shooting which included shots of the audience.

In February, Billy moved to a one-bedroom apartment in Nashville and the Achy Breaky line dance was mailed to high profile dance clubs across the U. S. where it quickly caught on. On April 6, the video for "Achy Breaky Heart" debuted on TNN and CMT. As a result, radio stations started to get requests for the song even though it wasn't officially released on radio till April 14th.

"Achy Breaky Heart" hit the number one spot on Billboard Hot Country Singles chart and became the top selling single of 1992. Billy's first album, Some Gave All, entered the Billboard Country Album charts at number one and sold twenty million copies worldwide. In the U.S., the album was certified nine times platinum, spent seventeen weeks at number one, and forty-three weeks in the top ten.

In 1993, Billy released his follow-up album, It Won't Be The Last, which debuted at number one on the Billboard Country charts, was certified platinum, and featured two top ten singles, "In the Heart of a Woman" and "Somebody New." Between 1994 and 1998, he released three albums, Storm in the Heartland (1994) which achieved gold status, his most critically acclaimed album Trail of Tears (1996), and Shot Full of Love (1998) which featured the single "Busy Man" that reached number three on the country charts.

Billy has appeared on *Top of the Pops*, *The Nanny*, and *Diagnosis Murder* as himself but credits his father for getting him into acting. Ron told Billy that he wanted him to have a career that stood the test of time and the way to do that was to get into television and films. Since Billy valued his father's opinion, he auditioned for David Lynch's film *Mulholland Drive* (2001) and got a small part. During filming, Lynch told Billy that he could be an actor if he just continued to be "real" like he was during filming of the movie.

The next week, Billy read about the TV show *DOC* that, according to Billy, represented hope, faith, and love. The show aired on the PAX TV network. Billy played Clint Cassidy, a country doctor, who moves to New York City for love but ends up heartbroken. Despite this, Cassidy decides to stay in New York and work for an HMO. The family friendly show won over fans and featured Billy's music including tracks from his album Southern Rain (2000).

From 2006 to 2011, Billy starred in the Disney TV show *Hannah Montana*. He played Robby Stewart, the father of Miley Stewart a.k.a. Hannah Montana who was played by his real-life daughter, Miley Cyrus. Since the show, Miley has continued to act and has had a music career of her own.

Billy has had guest appearances on numerous TV shows including *Phineas and Ferb* and *90210*. In 2005, he acted and danced in the live stage performance of *Annie Get Your Gun* in Toronto, Canada. In 2006, Billy performed "The Star Spangled Banner" at Game 5 of the World Series in St. Louis, Missouri.

Billy competed on the fourth season of *Dancing with the Stars*, in 2007, and was a fan favorite. Billy and his partner, Karina Smirnoff, finished in fifth place. One of the highlights of the show for Billy was when he looked across the dance floor and saw Muhammad Ali. During the Beck interview, Billy described the experience, "You know what? These judges are going to roast me no matter what I do, so I'm going to go see my hero. And right at the end of my dance, I went over and kind of squared up, started throwing some punches. And he put that fist up there and threw a couple punches back. And so while I stood there getting roasted by the judges, he kept throwing those punches. And I was like, 'Wow, that's Muhammad Ali.' And when we took a break, he came and gave me a big hug. And that was just, that was worth it all for me right there."

Billy's latest project is the CMT show *Still the King* in which he plays Vernon Brown a.k.a. Burnin' Vernon, a washed up one hit wonder working as an Elvis impersonator. After a drunken night, Vernon crashes into an old country church and is sentenced to community service. Through this, he pretends to be the congregation's new minister and learns that he has a teenage daughter. The show premiered on June 12, 2016.

Billy has won a number of awards and honors including two AMAs, a CMA for Single of the Year ("Achy Breaky Heart"), a World Music Award for World's Best New Artist, the Country

Music Cares Humanitarian Award, and the Congressional Medal of Honor Society's Bob Hope Award for Excellence in Entertainment.

In his spare time, Billy enjoys working out with weights and riding his four-wheeler. He has been married to his wife, Leticia "Tish," since December 1993 and is the father of six children.

Ashland, Kentucky

Ashland, Kentucky is the largest city within Boyd County and, according to the 2010 census, has a population of 21,684 residents. The city is located at the southern bank of the Ohio River.

In 1786, the Poage family migrated to Ashland from the Shenandoah Valley, Virginia via the Cumberland Gap. They built a homestead along the Ohio River and named it Poage's Landing. This area was also known as Poage Settlement and the developing community around it remained an extended-family affair until the mid-19th century.

In 1854, the name was changed to Ashland after Henry Clay's Lexington Estate and to reflect the growing industrial base within the city. The early industrial growth was due to Ohio's pig iron industry and, particularly, the 1854 charter of the Kentucky Iron, Coal, and Manufacturing Company by the Kentucky General Assembly. In 1856, the General Assembly formally incorporated the city.

Ashland is home to The Paramount Arts Center, a converted movie theater built in 1930, which is currently a venue for the arts including concerts and plays. Also located within the city is the Highlands Museum and Discovery Center and the Jesse Stuart Foundation, an organization that is dedicated to the preservation of the literary legacy of Jesse Stuart (a 20th century writer from Greenup County, Kentucky) and other Appalachian writers.

The Judds

The Judds are a country duo made up of Naomi and Wynonna Judd. The pair moved to Nashville, Tennessee, in 1979, in pursuit of a music career. In 1983, the duo signed a recording contract with RCA Records and released an extended play (EP), <u>Wynonna and Naomi</u>, with six songs including their first number one song, "Mama

He's Crazy." In 1984, The Judds released their first studio album, Why Not Me. All three singles from the album reached number one on the country charts.

In an interview with Greta Van Susteren, Wynonna described the memory of their first appearance at the Grand Ole Opry, "This is where we started out at eighteen. You know, the Highwaymen were sitting in here, Johnny Cash, sharing a dressing room with Dolly Parton, Loretta Lynn, and Tammy Wynette. Are you kidding me? You can't. It's country music, its community."

The Judds continued to record together until 1991, when Naomi left the duo because of health problems. During this time, they recorded five studio albums, one Christmas album, and released two Greatest Hits albums.

The Judds have reunited several times since 1991 for TV shows, recordings, promotion, and touring. This includes a performance at the Super Bowl XXVIII halftime show, Naomi singing harmony on Wynonna's 2004 single "Flies on the Butter (You Can't Go Home Again)," their 2011 Last Encore Tour, and the reality series *The Judds*. The duo reunited, for the first time in over four years, to perform a series of shows entitled Girls Night Out in Las Vegas, Nevada in October 2015.

The Judds have received numerous awards and honors including fourteen number one hits, six Top Ten hits, nine CMA awards, eight Billboard awards, five Grammy awards, and being inducted into the Kentucky Music Hall of Fame in 2011. Judd Plaza in Ashland is named after the duo and serves as the location for the city's Christmas tree and New Year's Eve ball drop.

Naomi Judd

Naomi Judd was born Diana Ellen Judd on January 11, 1946 in Ashland, Kentucky. She is the oldest of Charles and Pauline Judd's four children and grew up playing piano at church. At seventeen, she married Michael Ciminella and had a daughter, Christina Ciminella (Wynonna Judd). In 1968, Naomi and Wynonna moved to Los Angeles, California. Later that same year, her daughter, Ashley, was born.

Naomi and Michael divorced in 1972. In 1976, Naomi and her daughters moved back to Kentucky where they lived in a mountain home. During this time, Naomi studied nursing and would sing songs, ranging from bluegrass to showbiz, with Wynonna at the dinner table.

In 1979, Naomi and Wynonna moved to Tennessee, near Nashville, to pursue a music career. Naomi changed her name from Diana to Naomi, which she selected from a Bible story. The pair began to play music with Wynonna singing lead and playing guitar. While working as a hospital nurse and taking care of a patient who was related to label producer Brent Maher, Naomi managed to get an audition at RCA Records.

Naomi left the duo in 1991 after she was diagnosed with Hepatitis C. Since then, she has starred in the films *A Holiday Run* (1999) and *An Evergreen Christmas* (2014), hosted a Sunday morning talk show, *Naomi's New Morning,* which aired for two seasons, and joined the reality competition series *Can You Duet* (2008) as a judge/mentor. In addition to the awards the duo won together, Naomi won a Grammy for Best Country Song with "Love Can Build A Bridge" in 1991, along with Paul Overstreet and John Jarvis.

Today, Naomi is married to Larry Strickland and makes her home, outside of Nashville, in an area referred to as Peaceful Valley. Her daughters, Wynonna and Ashley, also have homes on the property.

Wynonna Judd

Wynonna Judd was born Christina Claire Ciminella on May 30, 1964 in Ashland, Kentucky. She is the daughter of Naomi Judd and Charles Jordan. In 1976, after moving back to Kentucky from Los Angeles, Wynonna learned to play a guitar she had received as a present. After moving to Tennessee, she attended Franklin High School (Franklin, Tennessee).

After graduation, Wynonna worked as a secretary while Naomi went to record companies on Music Row in an attempt to get a company interested in her daughter. Like her mother, Wynonna changed her name in 1979. Her new name was inspired from the lyrics, "Flagstaff Arizona, Don't Forget Winona," featured in the old swing song "Route 66." Winona is actually a small unincorporated community in the northern part of Arizona.

After her mother's departure from the duo in 1991, Wynonna embarked on a solo career. On January 27, 1992, she debuted the first single from her album, "She Is His Only Need." Her performance at the American Music Awards was the first time she sang solo on television. Her first album, Wynonna, released in March was certified five times platinum and featured three number one hit songs.

Wynonna's 1997 album The Other Side featured the song "Come Some Rainy Day" written by Billy Kirsch and Bat McGrath. Before her performance of the song at a concert in Kentucky on May 17, 2000, Wynonna told the crowd, "This song is very dear to my heart and I can't sing it without the one that inspired it." Her sister, Ashley, came out on stage and sat beside her throughout the performance. "Come Some Rainy Day" reached number fourteen on the Billboard Hot Country Singles & Tracks Chart in March 1998.

Wynonna continued her solo career with seven studio albums, a Christmas album, and three compilation albums. Her list of accomplishments includes three of her albums being certified platinum or higher, her fourth album being certified gold, and ten Top Ten hits.

Wynonna has had guest appearances on various television shows including *Hope & Faith* and as rock star Molly Cule in the cartoon *The Magic School Bus*. She released the memoir *Coming Home to Myself*, in 2005, which became a New York Times bestseller.

Wynonna's latest album, Wynonna & the Big Noise, is the first album she has recorded with a band instead of studio musicians. The album was released on February 12, 2016 and features vocalists including Timothy B. Schmit (of the Eagles) and Jason Isbell. Most of the project was recorded at Wynonna's family farm. She described the experience of making the album, "Like a garage band we all get in a room, basically knee to knee in a circle and jam until it feels amazing." According to Wynonna, the finished product is her favorite thing that she has done this far in her career.

Wynonna has a son, Elijah, and a daughter, Grace, from a previous relationship. She and her husband, Cactus Moser, have a home in Tennessee near Nashville.

Cordell, Kentucky

Located in Lawrence County, Cordell, Kentucky is an unincorporated community. The community was named after the Cordell family of settlers. The Cordell post office was established in 1898 and was in operation until 1975.

Larry Cordle

Larry Cordle, known to his friends as "Cord", was born on November 16, 1949. He was raised in Cordell, Kentucky on his family's small farm which had an outhouse and no electricity. In an interview with Tom Netherland, Larry discussed his childhood, "It was difficult but I wouldn't trade it for anything. Lord knows most any song I've written come from there." He continued, "I'm proud of my old Appalachian roots. My parents were God-fearing and hard-working. It was good for me. We never thought about being poor, but I guess we were."

By the time Larry was two years old, he could sing "I'll Fly Away" all the way through. He was introduced to bluegrass, country, and gospel music at a young age by his great grandfather, Harry Bryant, a dancer who played an old time clawhammer banjo and fiddle.

Larry has commented on his grandfather's influence, "We lived so far away from everything that we had to make our own entertainment. Papaw would get the fiddle out in the evenings sometimes and play and dance for us. Just as soon as I was old enough to try and learn to play I did so and kinda seconded him on his guitar. He ran an old country store and I spent many happy hours in there with him playing, talking about, and listening to music. It was our escape into another world, something we grew up with and looked so forward to. I was always happiest when we were in a jam session."

Growing up, Larry was friends with his neighbor Ricky Skaggs. In the Netherland interview, he spoke about their friendship, "Playing music was a big part of everybody's life. Other than playing like wild Indians, that's what we did around my house, Ricky Skaggs' house."

After high school graduation, Larry spent four years in the Navy. Upon receiving an honorable discharge, he attended Morehead State University (Morehead, Kentucky) where he earned his bachelors degree in Accounting. Larry was unsure of how he could make a living at music so he worked at a CPA firm in Paintsville, Kentucky during the day and played clubs at night.

Larry wanted a full time music career but his commitments kept him divided until Ricky Skaggs recorded and released his song "Highway 40 Blues." In the summer of 1983, the song became a number one hit and helped Larry get closer to his goal of working in music full time. In 1985, after receiving encouragement from Ricky, Larry gave up the stability of his job and moved to Nashville, Tennessee to work as a staff songwriter at Ricky's company, Amanda-Lin Music.

Larry spoke about this opportunity to work as a songwriter, "Two hundred bucks a week. That wouldn't go far these days but I made myself a promise that if I ever got a chance, one foot inside the door, that I was gonna work my behind off, as hard as I could to stay inside of it."

After the move, Larry wrote songs that were recorded by a number of country artists including "Against the Grain" by The Oak Ridge Boys, "Callin' Your Name" by Ricky Skaggs, "Hollywood Squares" by George Strait, and "Mama, Don't Forget To Pray For Me" by Diamond Rio. He has also had songs recorded by John Michael Montgomery, Allison Krauss, and Loretta Lynn.

In addition to being a songwriter, Larry has recorded several albums with his band Lonesome Standard Time including <u>Songs From the Workbench</u> (Ripchord/Shell Point Records, 2004), <u>Lynyrd Skynyrd Time: A Bluegrass Tribute to Lynyrd Skynyrd</u> (CMH Records, 2004), and <u>Took Down and Put Up</u> (Lonesome Day, 2007). His 1992 album <u>Lonesome Standard Time</u> (Sugar Hill Records) featured the song "Lonesome Standard Time" which won Song of the Year from the International Bluegrass Music Association. Members of Lonesome Standard Time include Terry Eldridge on upright bass, Booie Beech on lead acoustic guitar, Fred Carpenter on fiddle, David Harvey on mandolin, and David Talbot on banjo.

One of Larry's most notable songs is "Murder on Music Row" which originally appeared on Larry's 1999 album of the same title. The song is a criticism of the ongoing trend in country pop crossover acts and pop influence on country music. This trend has pushed traditional and new traditional music and artists to the fringe of country music. The lyrics metaphorically compare this trend to a horrible act: "That murder was committed down on music row." The song also references three traditional artists by their nicknames; Hank Williams as "Old Hank," Merle Haggard as "The Hag," and George Jones as "The Possum."

"Murder on Music Row" was performed by George Strait and Alan Jackson on the 1999 *CMA Awards Show*. They also recorded it for George's album Latest Greatest Straightest Hits. The studio version of the song was never officially released as a single but reached number thirty-eight on the Hot Country charts from unsolicited play. It also served as the b-side of George's 2000 single "Go On." George and Alan's version of the song won two CMA awards: Vocal Event of the Year (2000) and Song of the Year (2001). In 2006, Dierks Bentley and George Jones recorded a version of "Murder on Music Row" for the album Songs of the Year 2007.

Currently, Larry writes songs for his independent company, Wandachord Music. He continues to record music, tour, and occasionally provides background vocals for artists such as Blake Shelton.

In 2015, Larry was inducted into the Kentucky Music Hall of Fame. Him and his wife, Wanda, have one daughter, Kelvey, and live in Nashville. Even though he moved away years ago, Larry still enjoys returning to Eastern Kentucky for visits.

Ricky Skaggs

Ricky Lee Skaggs was born on July 18, 1954 in Cordell, Kentucky to Hobert and Dorothy May Skaggs. The couple raised their three sons and daughter in the Brushy Creek area. During the 2016 ASCAP awards, Ricky reflected on where he grew up, "I could have been born anywhere in the world, but God had a purpose for me to be born in Eastern Kentucky to hear the sounds of the mountains and the Stanley Brothers and Flatt & Scruggs and Bill Monroe."

Ricky grew up in a musical family and was influenced by his father and mother. Both of them were music lovers who particularly liked bluegrass and Ricky quickly adopted their tastes.

When Hobert was young, he would play guitar and sing with his brother, Okel, who played mandolin. Okel was killed in World War II so Hobert, devastated by the loss of his brother and musical partner, decided that if he ever had a son he would buy him a mandolin and pass on his brother's love for the instrument. When Ricky was young, his father recognized his talent and knew that the two of them could play music together.

As a young boy, Ricky would listen to the Grand Ole Opry and dream of having a career in music. In his book *Kentucky Traveler*, Ricky recalled the experience, "I used to go to sleep on my Papaw Skaggs' lap listening to the Opry on an old tube radio in his Ford pickup. To get a clear signal, we'd pull the truck away from the house where all the electric lines were hooked up and park down by the barn. He'd turn on the radio and work the knob to pick up the Opry broadcast on WSM. The radio frequency out of Nashville would come and go up in those mountains, so you had to sit there real quiet and wait for the music to break through the static. And then we'd hear Roy Acuff and Bill Monroe and it was the greatest sound in the world."

The Baptist church that the family attended was Ricky's first stage. He would sit on the pulpit and sing harmony with his mother when he was three years old. According to Ricky's brother, Garold Skaggs, Ricky was musical from a very young age and it seemed to him that Ricky always needed to be doing something with his hands.

At age five, his father, who was a pipe worker in New York, gave Ricky a Potato Bug Mandolin and showed him the G, C, and D chords. Two weeks later, Hobert returned home to discover that Ricky was making chord changes and singing along while playing. In an interview with Diane Rehm, Ricky described the experience of receiving his first mandolin, "And he [Hobert] was so smart, I think, to not start me on a guitar, something that was just huge for me. But this little mandolin became, you know how people, little kids would drag a blanket around, that mandolin was my blankie, okay? It was just everywhere I went, that mandolin went with me." Garold described why he would carry Ricky's mandolin at church, "He was so small, I'd hate to see him carry his mandolin. I would carry it for him, I was his first roadie."

By age six, Ricky was becoming something of a local celebrity. During a Bill Monroe concert, in Martha, Kentucky, the crowd insisted that 'Little Ricky Skaggs' perform onstage. Monroe, willing to oblige, placed his own mandolin around Ricky's neck and watched as he played and sang for the crowd.

Growing up, Ricky regularly performed with different individuals on a variety of stages including in front of Ralph and Carter Stanley at Blaine High School (Blaine, Kentucky). Ricky and his parents had a band, The Skaggs Family, and would enter local talent contests. According to Garold, the band came in first place and won fifty silver dollars at a contest in Morgan County, Kentucky.

In 1960, the family moved to Nashville, Tennessee in pursuit of Ricky's career. While there, Ricky attempted to perform at the Grand Ole Opry more than once but people weren't interested in having such a young child perform. He did, however, appear on the Flatt & Scruggs' Martha White Show when he was seven years old. Garold, who was at the studio that day, recalled the experience, "Ricky walked up to Lester and pulled on his coat tails and Lester looked down at him and said 'What do you want?' Ricky said 'I want to pick' so he performed a song called "Rudy"." He was paid $52.50 for his performance.

During that time, the show would broadcast in different towns on different nights so the family received a card letting them know what night it would air in Tennessee. That night, the family had an early dinner and settled in to watch the show. In the Rehm interview, Ricky recalled that evening, "We watched the first, you know, ten or fifteen minutes of the show and then they go to commercial and come back and that's when I was supposed to come out. And when I saw myself walk out on the television, I freaked out....back then, you know, in the early '60s and so just being from the mountains of Kentucky, you know, I just hadn't seen a lot of that. And of course, we were living in Goodlettsville, Tennessee. But when I saw myself, I ran into my bedroom and got under my bed." Ricky listened to his performance but didn't see the footage until many years later.

In the mid 1960s, the family moved back to Cordell. Ricky continued to perform including the Fall Carnival held each year in Blaine. According to Garold, these shows were fundraisers for the local school and people would pay an entrance fee of about fifty cents. Early on, Ricky performed with his parents but as he got older, he formed a band with his friends called The Untouchables.

When Ricky was fifteen, he met Keith Whitley while competing at a talent show in Ezel, Kentucky. The two boys ended up talking and getting to know each other in a downstairs locker room. Ricky recalled part of the conversation the two of them had in the Rhem interview, "So I said, well, who do you like? And, oh, I love the Stanley Brothers. Well, I love the Stanley Brothers too, you know. And so, do you know this song? And you know, yeah, and so we started singing and we ended up spending the next hour totally just alone, nobody else around, nobody to bother us. I mean, we just bonded immediately as brothers."

Keith invited Ricky to come and perform on the radio show he recorded with his brother Dwight Whitley each week. The next week, Ricky and his father came to the Whitley house and appeared on the show. Ricky became a regular on the show and, according to Dwight, the boys were able to influence each other musically.

In 1970, Ricky and Keith attended a Ralph Stanley show in Fort Gay, West Virginia. Ralph had a flat tire and was late so he called the club to let them know. The club owner knew that Ricky and Keith were there so he asked them if they had their instruments. They got on stage and started performing Stanley Brother songs.

In the Rehm interview, Ricky remembered the experience, "So we're playing there for, you know, fifteen, twenty minutes and in walks Ralph, my hero. And he doesn't go to the dressing room like I wish he had of. So he pulls up a bar stool and just sits over there, totally by himself and listens to us play. And in my peripheral vision, I can see him and I'm saying, please don't look at me, please don't listen to me. I was so shy and so embarrassed, you know. But that night really was a defining moment in my life because Ralph, he fell in love with me and Keith and asked us to come and do some shows with him, asked us to play on his break, get back up and play some more songs and so we bonded as friends. And so we worked the summer when we got out of high school. We worked that summer with him. And then we went back to school and finished up our senior year and Ralph hired us full time to go on the road and be Clinch Mountain Boys."

After leaving Stanley, Ricky became a member of many bands including The Country Gentlemen and J. D. Crowe & the New South. He formed Boone Creek, a progressive bluegrass band. Members of the band included Vince Gill and Jerry Douglas. Later, Ricky joined Emmylou Harris's Hot band for a few years where he sang harmony and played the mandolin and fiddle.

In 1981, Ricky made his major label debut with the album Waitin' for the Sun to Shine on Epic Records. The album produced two number one singles on the country charts, "Crying My Heart Out Over You" and "I Don't Care." In 1982, he became a member of the Grand Ole Opry. At that time, he was the youngest member to ever be inducted. Ricky continued his career throughout the 1980s with three consecutive number one country albums and a total of twelve number one hits.

In the 1990s, Ricky returned to his bluegrass roots. Along with his band, Kentucky Thunder, he continued to tour and release albums including My Father's Son (1991) and Solid Ground (1995). In 1997, Ricky launched his own record label, Skaggs Family Records, and released his first album on the new label, Bluegrass Rocks!.

During the 2000s and 2010s, he continued to record several albums with Kentucky Thunder, The Whites, and other musicians. In 2009, Ricky released his first solo album, Ricky Skaggs Solo: Songs My Dad Loved, where he celebrated his father, Hobert. To date, he has accumulated a number of prestigious awards including fourteen Grammys, eight CMAs, eight ACMs, and thirteen IBMAs (International Bluegrass Music Association).

Ricky continues to record albums and tour. In addition to the mandolin, he plays guitar, fiddle, mandocaster, and banjo. He lives in Tennessee with his wife, Sharon White, whom he married in 1981. Ricky has four children and two grandchildren.

River, Kentucky

River, Kentucky is an unincorporated community located in Johnson County. On September 6, 1890, the post office was established. River is home to the world's largest "plastic" bridge. The Forrest and Maxie Preston Memorial Bridge spans the Levisa Fork and connects River to the community of Offut. In 1999, River received international attention when the wooden deck of the 420-foot-long bridge was replaced with a deck of glass fiber-reinforced polymer composites. The previous record holder, the Aberfeldy Bridge in Scotland, was thirty feet shorter.

Hylo Brown

Frank "Hylo" Brown Jr. was born April 20, 1922 in River, Kentucky to Frank and Elizabeth Brown. He grew up in the Whalley Branch area and loved Appalachian music. Hylo didn't grow up in a musical home but got his start when his father bought him a three dollar guitar and a local music teacher gave him lessons. Hylo earned his nickname from Smokey Ward, a DJ at WPFB in Middletown, Ohio, due to his wide vocal range of high to low notes on the 1920s hillbilly hit "The Prisoner's Song."

Tommy Boyd, who played music with Hylo and is a current member of the Dry Branch Music Squad, remembered how his late father-in-law, Ernest Preston, and Hylo were born and raised within a mile or so of each other. According to Tommy, the two were friends and "Hylo used to bring his guitar over to the Preston farm and play and sing for hours on the porch for anyone who would listen." He continued by telling how Hylo and Ernest "went their separate ways when they left home and never met again. Ironically, those boyhood friends are now at rest within ten feet of each other in the Rose Hill Cemetery in Springfield, Ohio, some two hundred miles from River, Kentucky and ninety some years later."

In 1939, Hylo began his musical career at WMCI, a radio station in Ashland, Kentucky. Afterwards, he worked at a strip mine in West Virginia and on *Saturday Jamboree*, a radio show on WLOG (Logan, West Virginia). While living in West Virginia, he met his first wife, Bessie, whom he soon married. After getting married, the couple followed Hylo's parents to Springfield, Ohio where they had recently moved due to his father getting a factory job.

In Ohio, Hylo began writing and playing music on local radio broadcasts. One of his songs was a tribute to the Grand Ole Opry that was recorded by Jimmy Martin. In 1950, after a first place win during a talent contest, Hylo joined Bradley Kincaid's band at WWSO, a station Kincaid owned, in Springfield. After hearing a song that Hylo had wrote, Kincaid and DJ Tommy Sutton offered to help him meet people in Nashville, Tennessee.

In 1954, a copy of Hylo's song "Lost to a Stanger" was sent to Ken Nelson of Capital Records. Kitty Wells was set to record the song until Nelson offered Hylo a contract if he recorded it himself. Hylo decided to sign with the label and, in November, recorded his first songs. He stayed with Capital Records for three years.

In early 1955, Hylo formed the band Buckskin Boys and performed on *WWVA Jamboree* in Wheeling, West Virginia. In 1957, Hylo joined Lester Flatt and Earl Scruggs becoming a featured vocalist with the duo's Foggy Mountain Boys. Due to the increasing popularity of the group, Flatt & Scruggs decided to form a second Foggy Mountain Band. The Buckskin Boys were renamed The Timberliners with Hylo as lead singer. During this time, Hylo, his wife, and children moved to Nashville for over three years.

The Timberliners began performing on television stations in Tennessee and Mississippi and later in West Virginia after they started switching schedules with Flatt & Scruggs. In 1958, the album Hylo Brown and the Timberliners was released. As technology increased, the original Flatt & Scruggs band was able to be videotaped and appear on multiple television stations. This advancement effectively ended the career of the Timberliners.

However, Hylo decided to rejoin Flatt & Scruggs as a featured singer.

During the 1960s, Hylo recorded and released several solo albums including Bluegrass Balladeer (1961), Bluegrass Goes to College (1962), and Folk Songs of Rural America (1967). In the late 1960s, Hylo met fellow musician Tommy Boyd. Both of them were working in south central Ohio when a guitar player that Tommy knew arranged for the two of them to be part of Hylo's backup band. They mostly performed at small venues and square dances.

Additionally, they performed at a Grand Ole Opry package show at the Memorial Hall in Springfield with George Jones and Skeeter Davis. According to Tommy, "Hylo Brown was a true country troubadour who had a life-long love for his music. Hylo was fun to work with and had his own material, along with many old standards. He was very professional and was a great emcee with a lot of country humor. He liked to do most of the driving, and the more he talked, the faster he drove!"

In 1970, Hylo was semi-retired, due to his health, and settled back home in Whalley Branch with his second wife, Elizabeth. He continued to do limited shows, including some where his son, Tim Brown, joined him on stage. In 1992, a two-CD compilation, Hylo Brown and the Timberliners, was released.

In 1991, Hylo moved to Springfield to be near his family. He passed away on January 17, 2003 in Mechanicsburg, Ohio and is buried in Rose Hill Burial Park in Springfield. He is survived by his son, three daughters, a cousin whom he helped raise, eleven grandchildren, and four great-grandchildren. Tim and his sisters, Candy and Vickie, stated "that they love and miss their father and mother."

Hylo was inducted into the Grand Ole Opry in 1959. According to Tim, his father considered the fact that he was an Opry member for forty-five years to be one of his biggest accomplishments. Tim fondly remembers going to the Opry with his father and meeting artists including Grandpa Jones and Minnie Pearl.

Hylo's musical reach expands beyond the United States. Tim recalled being stationed in Germany and how the citizens were impressed that his father was Hylo Brown since they were fans of his waltz-style of music.

Hylo and his music are still remembered and recognized today. Bill Purk, a fellow musician who helped organize an event in Ohio to honor Hylo, said that he was affected by Hylo "as he was the last of his generation, a pioneer." Floyd Alexander played music with Hylo and stated, "He was as good of a storyteller as he was a singer and player." Hylo's 1958 Capital Records album <u>Hylo Brown and the Timberliners</u> is on display at the Smithsonian in Washington D.C.

Van Lear, Kentucky

Located in Johnson County, Van Lear, Kentucky is a small, unincorporated community and former coal town. Originally, John Caldwell Calhoun Mayo bought the coal rights to land along Miller's Creek and later sold it to Northern Coal and Coke. It was later acquired by Consolidated Coal Company (Consol). The town was named for one of Consol's directors, Van Lear Black, and was incorporated in 1912.

Five miles of railroad were built on the Johnson County property by Consol using money loaned by Van Lear Black's Fidelity Trust. Within Van Lear, five underground coal mines were opened and operated from 1910 to 1946. During the boom times of these mines, the population of Van Lear was over 4,000 and included local miners, Appalachians, and immigrant Irish and Italians since the mines were integrated.

Consol merged with the Pittsburgh Coal Company in 1945 and then disposed of its Miller Creek properties. Those living in company-owned housing were offered first chance at purchasing the homes which many choose to do. Most of the major buildings were torn down.

Loretta Lynn

Loretta Webb Lynn was born on April 14, 1932 and was named after film star Loretta Young. She was the second child of Theodore "Ted" and Clara "Clary" Webb's eight children and was raised in a cabin in Butcher Hollow, Van Lear, Kentucky. Her father was a coal miner who worked nights at the Van Lear mine and spent his days working the fields. Her younger sister, Brenda Gail Webb, also became a singer performing under the name Crystal Gayle.

Growing up, Loretta regularly sang at churches and local concerts. She was raised in a musical family and has described her childhood by saying, "When I was growing up with my sisters and brothers, we all sang and rocked the babies to sleep but that was as far as we ever did." As a child, Loretta enjoyed climbing trees and would make her own toys to play with.

In an interview with Gary Chapman, Loretta discussed her upbringing and how it influenced her. She stated, "I'm glad that it was hard for me. I'm glad that I learned. When I left Butcher Hollow, after I left, I knew that things were worse than I knew at the time. I'm glad that life's been hard for me all the way. Cause we've all got a better place to go someday. Well, but, you know I don't think people really work hard at what they do if they come from a family that's got it all together."

At age fifteen, she met Oliver "Doo" Lynn, twenty-one, and married him a month later in January 1948. Loretta had never planned to leave Butcher Hollow but followed Doo to Washington where he hoped to find a job outside of the coal mines. After a year of marriage, Doo and Loretta, who was seven months pregnant, moved to the logging community of Custer, Washington.

After getting married, Loretta stopped singing publicly and focused on her family. She passed on a love of music to her children by singing songs that her mother had taught her including "In The Pines" and "The Great Titanic." By the time she was twenty, Loretta had two sons, Jack and Benny, and two daughters, Betty and Clara.

In 1953, Doo bought Loretta a Harmony guitar for seventeen dollars as an anniversary present. During the next three years, Loretta, who was self-taught, worked on improving her playing. She started her own band, Loretta and the Trailblazers, with encouragement from Doo. The band which included her younger brother, Jay Lee, on lead guitar often played at clubs near her Washington home.

Loretta won a televised talent contest in Tacoma, Washington hosted by Buck Owens. The prize for winning the contest was a wristwatch that broke a day later; Loretta later laughed about it with

Buck. Her performance was seen by Norm Burley, co-founder of Zero Records, who created the label with the sole purpose of recording Loretta.

Loretta signed a contract with Zero Records on February 2, 1960. Dan Grashey, president of the label, set up recording sessions in Hollywood where Loretta recorded four of her own compositions. Later that year, the Lynns began promoting her first single, "I'm a Honky Tonk Girl," by traveling across the country stopping at country music stations urging them to play the song. Additionally, thousands of copies were mailed out to radio stations. The song climbed to number fourteen on the country music charts and caught the attention of the Wilburn Brothers. They hired Loretta to tour with them and the family moved to Nashville, Tennessee in late 1960.

Loretta began cutting demos for Teddy and Doyle Wilburn's publishing company. One of these demos "Biggest Fool of All" wrote by Kathryn Fulton attracted the attention of Owen Bradley, a producer at Decca Records. Bradley wanted the song for artist Brenda Lee so the Wilburns worked out a deal, Lee could have the song if Decca would sign a deal with Loretta.

Starting in 1960, Loretta began appearing on the Grand Ole Opry and became a member on September 25, 1962. The same year, she released her first single on Decca records, "Success," which reached number six on the country charts. Loretta was on her way to becoming a top female country artist.

Loretta met fellow Decca artist Patsy Cline who became Loretta's close friend and mentor. About the friendship, Loretta said, "She taught me a lot about how to dress. She told me to get out of the jeans. 'Course, I'd wear them till we got to the radio station and then I'd get in the backseat and put on my dress. And I'd take the dress off and go back into my jeans and go to the next radio station." In 1964, Loretta had twin daughters, Peggy and Patsy, the latter being named after Patsy Cline.

Beginning with her 1966 single, "You Ain't Woman Enough," Loretta began writing songs from a feminist point of view. Songs had themes such as philandering husbands, persistent mistresses, double standards for men and women with the song "Rated X," birth control with the song "The Pill," and repeated childbirth with the song "Ones On The Way." Some country radio stations refused to play her music and banned nine of her songs.

In the Chapman interview, Loretta explained that she was just writing and singing about life, not the women's liberation movement. She also explained her reaction to the controversy, "I really didn't think about it being wrong when I would sing them and record them. I didn't know that people would think that they were a little wrong. I really didn't know any better. Maybe I would have thought about it twice if I would have known but I didn't." She added that she's glad she didn't know.

Despite the bans, Loretta went on to become one the most successful female artists of the time. Her single "Don't Come Home A' Drinkin' (With Lovin' on Your Mind)," from the album of the same title, became Loretta's first song to reach number one on the Billboard Country charts. Loretta co-wrote the song with her sister Peggy Sue Webb.

In 1971, Loretta and Conway Twitty partnered up to become one of the most successful duos in country history. Loretta and Conway had five consecutive number ones, seven Top Ten hits, and were named the CMA Vocal Duo of the Year four years in a row (1972-1975).

Loretta released her autobiography, *Coal Miner's Daughter*, written by herself and George Vecsey in 1976. In March 1980, the movie *Coal Miner's Daughter*, starring Sissy Spacek as Loretta and Tommy Lee Jones as Mooney (Doo), was released and became a number one box office hit. The film was nominated for and won multiple awards and honors including two Golden Globes, a gold album for the soundtrack, and four Oscars including a Best Actress Award for Spacek.

Loretta released the album I Remember Patsy, in 1977, which was dedicated to Patsy Cline who had died in a 1963 plane crash. It covered some of Patsy's biggest hits. Lynn released two singles from the album, "She's Got You" which reached number one and "Why Can't He Be You" which was a top ten hit. She released the album Honky Tonk Angels with Dolly Parton and Tammy Wynette in 1993.

In 1995, at the 30th Academy of Country Music Awards, Loretta was presented with the Pioneer Award. Doo passed away the next year. In 2000, her first album in several years, Still Country, was released and included a tribute song to her late husband, "I Can't Hear the Music."

Released in 2004, Loretta's album Van Lear Rose was produced by Jack White, of the White Stripes, whom Loretta referred to as "a kindred spirit." While talking about Loretta, Jack said, "I want as many people as possible on Earth to hear her because she's the greatest female singer-songwriter of the last century."

Loretta either wrote or co-wrote every song on the album and Jack's guitar work and background vocals were featured. This collaboration with Jack allowed Loretta to reach new audiences and generations. Loretta and Jack won two Grammys for their work including the award for Best Country Album of the Year.

In 2010, Sony Music released a tribute album entitled Coal Miner's Daughter: A Tribute to Loretta Lynn. The album featured artists including Kid Rock, Sheryl Crow, Alan Jackson, The White Stripes, Martina McBride, Paramore, and Steve Earle.

On March 4, 2016, Loretta released the album Full Circle which featured new music, new versions of her hits, and county standards with guest vocals from Willie Nelson and Elvis Constello. The album debuted at number nineteen on the Billboard 200 all genre chart.

Loretta continues to tour and owns a ranch in Hurricane Mills which is billed as the seventh largest attraction in Tennessee. The ranch features a recording studio, museums, lodging, western stores, restaurants, and other attractions. There are normally three holiday concerts held there each year on Memorial Day weekend, the 4th of July weekend, and Labor Day weekend. The ranch also includes a replica of her parent's cabin in Butcher Hollow and the home where the Lynns raised their children.

Throughout her lengthy career, Loretta has received numerous awards, accolades, and honors making her the most awarded female country recording artist. This list includes sixteen number one hits on the Billboard country charts (both for her solo and duet work), a Grammy Lifetime Achievement Award, and being the first woman to ever win CMA Entertainer of the Year. In addition, she has been inducted into the Country Music Hall of Fame (1983), the Kentucky Music Hall of Fame (2002), and the Songwriters Hall of Fame (2008).

Crystal Gayle

Crystal Gayle was born Brenda Gail Webb on January 9, 1951 in Paintsville, Kentucky. She was the youngest child of Theodore "Ted" and Clara "Clary" Webb's eight children and the only one born in a hospital. Crystal lived in Butcher Hollow, Van Lear, Kentucky until the age of four when the family moved to Wabash, Indiana. Crystal, a shy child, enjoyed listening to the radio and, with encouragement from her mother, would sing for visitors to their home.

Crystal grew up in a musical family and learned to play guitar since she was inspired by her older sister Loretta Lynn's musical success. Her mother taught all of her children a song about the Titanic that she had learned in grammar school. In an interview with Sports and Entertainment Nashville, Crystal remembered her childhood experiences, "When I was about four years old we moved from Kentucky to Indiana and everybody would get out on the porch and play guitar or the banjo."

While in junior high, Crystal and her sister, Peggy, would perform at different places around town. The girls would wear the stage clothes that Loretta had handed down to them. Their mother would alter the clothes to make them a better fit.

Crystal sang back-up in her brothers' folk band and, while in high school, began to tour with Loretta for a few weeks each summer. When Crystal was fifteen or sixteen, she made her first appearance on the Grand Ole Opry. She described the experience to Country Stars Central, "My first time to perform on the Opry, Loretta was sick and she talked them into letting me perform in her spot. I remember singing "Ribbon of Darkness Over Me" in my little shiny dress my mother made me."

After graduating from Wabash High School, Crystal signed a deal with Decca Records. Decca already had a singer named Brenda Lee so Crystal was asked to change her name. In an interview conducted at the Thunder Valley Resort, she described how Loretta came up with her new name, "Well you know in the south, we have some hamburgers that are called a chain, that's a hamburger chain that are called Krystals so that's where she saw it. But she said since you are bright and shining that's what I want you called." As a result, Brenda Gail Webb became Crystal Gayle. During an appearance on *Pop Goes the Country*, Crystal told Ralph Stanley, "At the time, I really didn't care what my name was, I was going to record and that thrilled me."

During the earlier part of Crystal's career, Loretta wrote many of her songs including her first single, "I've Cried (The Blue Right Out Of My Eyes)." It was released in 1970 and sang in a similar style to that used by Loretta. The song reached number twenty-three on the Billboard County Music charts. Crystal would drive around Nashville hoping to hear the song on her car radio.

At this time, Crystal was regularly appearing on Blake Emmon's show, *The Country Place*, but was struggling to become an established artist. Decca requested that she record more songs that sounded like Loretta's recordings. Feeling frustrated, Crystal left Decca Records and signed with United Artists in 1974.

She began working with producer Alan Reynolds who offered her the creative freedom she wanted and helped her develop her own style. In an interview with CMT, Crystal discussed the advice she received from Loretta, "She told me that I should not sing her songs anymore when I started recording. She didn't want me to sound anything like her because she knew that I would not make it in this business trying to be another Loretta Lynn. And I think that is one of the main reasons that I choose a little bit more MOR (middle-of-the-road), you know easy listening style of county, and really she pushed me in that direction."

Crystal's self-titled album on United Artists was released and produced a Top Ten hit. In 1976, Crystal achieved her first number one on the country charts and made her first appearance on the Billboard Top 100 with her single "I'll Get Over You."

Alan believed that Crystal was in a position to make a large breakthrough and encouraged her to record the jazz flavored ballad "Don't It Make My Brown Eyes Blue." Crystal discussed the song in an interview with Gary James, "Oh, I loved it. I really like listening to Richard Lee's own recordings that he makes of himself and I've always loved his voice. I mean, he's such a great songwriter. I've always loved the way his style fit mine. Of course I would have said yes, I want that song." The song spent four weeks at number one on the Billboard Country charts, hit number two on the Billboard Top 100, and was the most successful song of her career. In 1978, the song won Crystal the Grammy Award for the Best Female Country Vocal Performance.

In 1982, Crystal worked on the soundtrack for the movie *One From the Heart*. The same year, she signed with Elektra Records and recorded the duet "You and I" with label mate Eddie Rabbit. The song, featured on Eddie's Radio Romance album, quickly went to number one on the country charts and number seven on the pop charts. Crystal's new album, True Love, produced three number one hits.

In 1985, Crystal recorded a duet with Gary Morris for the soundtrack of the television show *Dallas*. The song "Makin' Up For Lost Time (The Dallas Lover's Song)" hit the top of the country charts. Crystal and Gary teamed up again to record the duet album What If I Fall In Love (1987) which included the single "Another World." The song was used as the theme song for the television soap opera *Another World* until 1996. Crystal appeared on an episode of the show where she played herself.

In the 1990s, Crystal varied from the type of albums she had previously recorded including two gospel albums, Someday (1995) and He Is Beautiful (1997), a children's album, In My Arms (2003), and two live albums, Crystal Gayle in Concert (2006) and Live! An Evening With Crystal Gayle (2007).

Throughout her career, Crystal has received many awards and honors including four ACMs, two CMAs, eighteen Billboard number one country singles, six gold albums, and the distinction of becoming the first female artist in country music history to have a platinum album with We Must Believe In Magic (1977). In February 2008, she was inducted into the Kentucky Music Hall of Fame.

In October 2009, Crystal received a star on the Hollywood Walk of Fame. In the Thunder Valley interview, Crystal described the experience of seeing the Walk of Fame, "Oh, it was incredible because one of my first trips to California, to Los Angeles, was I stayed in Hollywood. And that was my first trip out; I went out to see the stars, to see the walk." There is only one star separating Crystal and Loretta's stars.

Crystal, who is known for her nearly floor length hair, still continues to perform and tour. She has been married to her husband, Bill Gatzimos, since 1971.They have two children, Chris and Catherine, and one grandson.

Prestonsburg, Kentucky

Prestonsburg, Kentucky is located in Floyd County and has a population 3,255, according to the 2010 census. The Prestonsburg area was part of the 100,000-acre tract of land that was granted to the family of Col. John Preston's wife. Col. Preston administered the land on her behalf. The grant was intended to permit British colonization beyond the Blue Ridge Mountains but its impact was limited due to subsequent French and Indian resistance and a reversal of British policy.

The land was settled when John Spurlock of Montgomery County, Virginia arrived in 1791 and outlaid Preston's Station in 1797. Upon its formation in 1799, it became the county seat and was formally established in 1818. Upon its establishment in 1816, the post office was known as the Floyd County Court House. It was renamed Prestonsburg in the late 1820s.

The area's role in the Civil War is evident by the Middle Creek National Battlefield which was the site of the largest and most significant battle in Eastern Kentucky, which took place on January 10, 1862.

Prestonsburg is home to the Mountain Arts Center which hosts concerts and the Kentucky Opry. The Jenny Wiley Theatre hosts theatrical productions throughout the year. Also located within the city is the East Kentucky Science Center which opened in 2004. The center is a private, non-profit science center and planetarium that is located on the main campus of Big Sandy Community and Technical College. In the fall of 2011, the Planetarium received a $200,000.00 grant making it one of the most technologically advanced Planetariums in the country. The center also features an exhibit hall with traveling exhibits, science classrooms, and a gift shop.

Sundy Best

Sundy Best is a duo comprised of Nick Jamerson and Kris Bentley. Their music is a blend of country, Appalachian folk, bluegrass, rock, soul, and R&B. Nick provides lead vocals and plays acoustic guitar while Kris plays drums.

Both Nick and Kris grew up in Prestonsburg, Kentucky. In an interview with WSAZ's Tim Irr, which was conducted before a concert to benefit Johnson County flood victims, Nick described Johnson County (which borders Floyd County) as "an area that obviously we grew up in, that nurtured us growing up, and nurtured us into adulthood and into our careers."

Both of the boys come from musical families. In an interview with Rich Copley, Nick described how music was a part of Thanksgiving and Christmas at his grandfather's house, "My grandfather would play banjo, my grandmother would play guitar, my great-aunt would play mandolin, the doctor from up the road would come and play fiddle, and it's just this big bluegrass lineup in the living room."

At nine years old, Nick started performing at church where his mother was the children's choir director. Today, he plays piano, guitar, banjo, and mandolin.

Kris's father plays guitar and sings so it was expected that he would too. In an interview with Chris Parton, Kris discussed his childhood musical influences, "Music is really the only thing in that town. Everyone plays and it's very rich in talent. We tell people all the time we're some of the less-talented people in that area. If you go there, six or seven people out of ten can probably pick up an instrument and play. It's just part of the culture, family get-togethers and church, something fun to do."

Kris discussed his and Nick's musical influences in an interview with Mark Petty, "Yeah, I mean we're kind of old school. You know, we grew up listening to the '70's classic rock. Our parents were always listening to Bob Seger, Tom Petty, The Eagles, The Allman Brothers. I remember learning to play the drums along to a Grand Funk Railroad album. Savoy Brown album...J. Geils Band. That's when we fell in love with music. That's what we were listening to. That's the kind of music we still listen to today, and what influences us and inspires us. Of course we listen to other stuff, too. But we're really into music that was relevant thirty years ago and will be relevant thirty years from today. Good music has no expiration date." Both Nick and Kris have been inspired by shows they attended at the Mountain Arts Center, in Prestonsburg, including Montgomery Gentry, Charlie Daniels, and Brad Paisley.

In an interview with CMT's Samantha Stephens, Nick discussed his and Kris's friendship, "We grew up together, we lived about three miles apart. We went to separate grade schools but played sports against each other and went to high school together and then played basketball together."

During their senior year in high school, the pair began playing music together on Sundays at church. In the Stephens interview, Kris discussed this experience, "We were in a Christian rock group in high school called Crosswalk." He continued, "We toured around the churches of Eastern Kentucky." In an interview with Preshias Harris, Kris described their experience with music in church, "Growing up in church, with church bands, we wrote songs, played music, and then you sang the songs." Nick added, "Whether they were good or not."

In an interview with Amber Philpott, Nick discussed the impact that church had on the duo, "We started a lot of our music in church, it was really our only outlet for us to play. That was a pretty important part of our life growing up, church was a big deal. I played drums at church all through school."

After graduating from high school in 2005, the boys went their separate ways. Nick went to the University of Pikeville (Pikeville, Kentucky) on a football scholarship where he studied history. While there, his favorite football coach introduced him to live music. In the Harris interview, Nick described how it inspired him, "The musicians I met inspired me. I found myself writing music. My life took a new direction." He also took voice lessons and spent a lot of time in his dorm room writing including the duo's song "My Friends and Me."

Kris attended Centre College in Danville, Kentucky where he played basketball and studied English. After graduation in 2010, Nick returned home and wanted to buy some drums. He called Kris who had no drums to sell but offered to play drums for Nick and another musician friend of theirs. They began performing around

Eastern Kentucky including Lexington where they had moved to in August.

They originally performed under the name Nick and Kris but quickly changed it to Sundy Best. The name was inspired by the term "Sunday best" clothing for church on Sundays which is the only place to publically play music in Prestonsburg. In the Parton interview, Kris explained the spelling change, "Sundy is how people say it back home. Sundy, Mondy, Tuesdy, so we spelt it how we talk. We go places and people are like, 'Where are you from? Louisiana?' I tell 'em South America." In the Copley interview, Nick explained, "It's weird saying Sunday." To which, Kris added, "It's like there's an extra syllable in there."

When the duo was formed, Kris played a drum set but downsized to a cajon due to space limitations at some venues. A cajon is a Peruvian instrument that is a portable box that the player sits on and slaps with their bare hands. In the Parton interview, Kris described his experience playing the cajon, "I saw a video of a guy with a Cajon and was like, 'That's cool. I need to go get me one of those.' We messed around with it that weekend and it was cool. I play it really hard, though, and I've been through like thirty drums or so. Never watched an instructional video!"

The duo recorded their first album <u>Tales, Lies, and Exaggerations</u> at home. In December 2011, the duo funded their first studio album by raising $15,000.00 through Kickstarter, a crowdsourcing website. The album, <u>Door Without a Screen</u>, was released in the summer of 2012.

The duo was asked by a mutual friend of a friend to be in a video that was being shot for Bucky Covington and Shooter Jennings, both of whom were on the record label eOne. They were introduced to Van Fletcher who became their future manager. Nick and Kris signed with eOne Music who released a deluxe version of <u>Door Without a Screen</u> on August 27, 2013.

In the Harris interview, Nick discussed the duo's original expectations and their record deal, "We never set out to get discovered or to be famous and get a deal. We set out to write our songs and sing. It's what we know, do, and love. The record deal was the right thing to do. It wasn't forced, just simply happened." Kris added, "We were happy just playing in and around Kentucky." He continued, "I think we're going to make the best music we possibly can; genuine music from where the heart is and see where we go from there."

Sundy Best's second studio album, <u>Bring up the Sun</u>, was released on March 10, 2014 and featured fifteen songs including remakes of "Home," Lilly," and "These Days." The album, produced by R.S. Fields, reached number eleven on the Billboard Top Country Album charts, number seventy on the Billboard 200, and sold 5,000 copies during the first week. The duo filmed videos for "These Days" and "Until I Met You."

<u>Salvation City</u>, the duo's third studio album, was released on December 2, 2014 and was named on Rolling Stone's 2014 list of 40 Best Albums. It debuted at number twenty-two on the Top Country Albums chart. The duo filmed the video for the single "Four Door" in their hometown of Prestonsburg.

Nick described the inspiration for the title, "Even with social media, I don't think the world is in any worse shape than it ever has been, but it can really bring you down, if you're always on Facebook and Twitter and constantly connected. I found the only time we could really escape it was at our shows, when we were working. It's like we were creating this little separate environment away from all the negative stuff, so that's where we came up with 'Salvation City.' It's whatever in your life that's an escape from the nonsense that's out there, if that keeps you sane, that's your 'Salvation City'."

The album featured new musical styles and electrical instrumentation. Their 2015 tour featured the additions of Kris on a full drum kit, Nick on electric guitar, and a keyboardist. The pair was joined on tour by Stan Nickell and Teddy Weckbacher.

Sundy Best calls their fans "kinfolk" since it has that down home family feel. In the Copley interview, Nick discussed how Kentucky influenced their work and the difference between their first and second album, "The first one was very Kentucky-centric. For the first time in our lives, we were missing Eastern Kentucky and things we took for granted. So it was very Kentucky-centric. This one, there will still be references only people in Kentucky are going to get. But it's a lot more broad, and it's going to open up some doors for us."

The duo has performed on the Grand Ole Opry multiple times, had videos on CMT, and songs on satellite radio. In February 2015, Sundy Best was added to the Country Music Highway. About the honor, Nick and Kris said, "When you think you cannot be humbled anymore, you see your name on a sign on the revered Country Music Highway. 'We were speechless' as we came up on the stretch of Highway U.S. 23. We are so proud to be two boys from Prestonsburg, Kentucky and we are so honored to have Sundy Best displayed proudly and infinitely in this way."

Additionally, Prestonsburg Mayor Les Stapleton presented Nick and Kris with the "keys to the city" in front of the Mountain Arts Center. At the presentation, the duo remarked, "Can we wake up now? This has been a weekend we will never forget and will hold dear in our hearts." They continued, "We appreciate our loyal fans, family, and friends that have supported us from the very beginning when this was just a dream. Thank you."

Betsy Layne, Kentucky

Betsy Layne, Kentucky is a Floyd county community located on the Levisa Fork of the Big Sandy River about thirteen miles southeast of Prestonsburg. It began on the Layne farm in the early nineteenth century and was named for Betsy Layne. The Chesapeake and Ohio Railroad arrived about 1908 and the Betsy Layne post office opened that year. The post office moved several times over the years. The original location became known as Justell but was later reabsorbed by a growing Betsy Layne. The population in 2010 was 688.

Dwight Yoakam

Dwight David Yoakam was born on October 23, 1956 in Pikeville, Kentucky. He is the oldest child of David and Ruth Ann Yoakam. Dwight has a sister, Kimberly, and a brother, Ronald. When Dwight was very young, the family moved to Columbus, Ohio. After his parent's divorce, Dwight lived with his mother and stepfather. His father, a gas station owner, also remarried.

Dwight grew up in a religious home and was taught to read the King James Version of the Bible. The family attended the Church of Christ. After the move, the family regularly traveled from Columbus to Betsy Layne, Kentucky where Dwight's grandparents, Luther and Earlene Tibbs, lived. In the book *Shuck Beans, Stack Cakes, and Honest Fried Chicken* by Ronni Lundy, Dwight fondly remembered, "My granny would come to the back porch with a big laundry basket full of beans. Friends gathered, and we would sit down and snap 'em and string 'em and crack 'em and throw 'em in the pan. We would sit there snapping and stringing for the whole afternoon. It could become a social event complete with fiddle or guitar music with singing."

Dwight attended Northland High School (Columbus, Ohio) where he excelled in music and drama. He acted in school plays including playing "Charlie" in *Flowers for Algernon* and Helen Keller's brother in *The Miracle Worker*. Outside of school, Dwight sang and performed with local garage bands and would entertain his friends with impersonations of people such as Richard Nixon. After graduating from high school in 1974, Dwight briefly attended Ohio State University.

In 1976, he decided to leave school so he could pursue a music career and moved to Nashville, Tennessee for a short time. After being told that his brand of "hillbilly honky-tonk" wasn't marketable, he moved to Los Angeles, California in 1977. In an interview with Kyle Meredith, Dwight described the experience of moving, "I'd been to Nashville the previous year and back and forth, and in those years it wasn't really what was going to deliver me to realize any ability to make a living doing and succeed at being a musical performer. So the beacon for me at that point was really, in a singular sense, was Emmylou Harris on the West Coast. And then peripherally Buck Owens and Merle Haggard. I was beginning to really be influenced by Merle's adult writing and Buck's effervescence and the style of things. And then I got to the West Coast in '77 and knew fairly quickly that it was going to be home. A musical home, and artistic home, and that's what it became."

Dwight began playing in the country music clubs but eventually moved to the rock clubs. The origins of his musical style came from his childhood. In an interview with Travis Smiley, Dwight stated, "Being born in rural Appalachia, in southeast Kentucky, bluegrass but more mountain music was in my DNA." During this time, he also drove air freight and was a bank courier.

Dwight teamed up with his first producer and lead guitarist, Pete Anderson, who came from a similar background since his family had also moved north for work. The two worked together on Dwight's first album Guitars, Cadillacs, Etc., Etc. Dwight wrote the songs and Pete worked on the arrangements and production. The finances for the six song EP (extended play) came from multiple sources; Dwight's sister and brother-in-law, an insurance check meant to fix his El Camino, and a benefit classical concert organized by UCLA professor Dr. Robert Winter.

In 1984, the traditional country album was released and Dwight went on tour with artists such as Los Lobos and Violent Femmes. While on tour, he gained an eclectic fan base that caught the attention of Warner Brothers. In 1986, Dwight signed to their Reprise Record label.

Reprise Records re-released <u>Guitars, Cadillacs, Etc., Etc.</u> with several additional songs added. The album reached number one on Billboard Top Country Albums Chart. The first single, "Honky Tonk Man," reached number three and was the first country music video ever played on MTV. His second single, "Guitars and Cadillacs," was inspired by his trips from Ohio to Betsy Layne and the fact that his aunt was the first person in his family to get a Cadillac. The song reached number four on the charts.

Dwight's grandfather, Luther Tibbs, passed away in 1979 after working in the coal mines for forty years. After attending the funeral, Dwight returned to Los Angeles and wrote "Miner's Prayer." It was featured on <u>Guitars, Cadillacs, Etc., Etc.</u> and was one of the earliest songs he wrote about Kentucky. During his induction into the Kentucky Music Hall of Fame, Dwight described how that the song was "in memorial to him [Luther] specifically but and in memorial to every man who ever crawled down in a coal mine with a pick and a shovel, later with tools, to pick out a living for themselves and their family."

The song "South of Cincinnati" is also included on the <u>Guitars, Cadillacs, Etc., Etc.</u> album. During the Meredith interview, Dwight described his inspiration for the song, "I remember the day that I left Louisville (Kentucky). I had been here visiting my dad; this was 1982. I had been down in Nashville pitching some songs, and I was driving his truck up to Ohio to visit my mom. She was there in Columbus. And I crested I-71 where it breaks to drop down at Covington and Newport, Kentucky into Cincinnati, and it's a beautiful vista from that hill on I-71 as you go. And daylight out through there, and it was just the right time of day, and the river was reflecting."

Dwight continued, "I wrote the song "South of Cincinnati" after I got back to California thinking about that drive, that day, seeing that river, seeing those places that were so much a part of my childhood. I mean, that river we crossed many times. Tail-light babies headed back to Kentucky you know, from Ohio, Michigan license plates. On that, further east, over by Ashland Route 23 out of Columbus, Ohio. It went from Detroit down through the center part of the state and crossed over to Ashland and would drive what they now dub 'the country music highway'."

Dwight's follow up album, Hillbilly Deluxe (1987) was just as successful as Guitar, Cadillacs, Etc., Etc. and included the single "Readin', Rightin', Route 23." The song was inspired by Dwight's childhood move to Ohio from Kentucky. Route 23 runs north from Kentucky through Columbus and Toledo, Ohio and into Michigan near the automotive factories. Instead of the traditional line used in elementary schools of the three R's, Readin', Rightin', 'Rhitmetic, Kentuckians used to say the three R's they learned were Readin', Rightin', Route 23. The expression was used to describe the route people would take to find a job outside of the coal mines. According to the Hillbilly Deluxe CD jacket, "Readin', Rightin', Route 23" was "Written for and lovingly dedicated to my mother, Ruth Ann; to my aunts, Margaret, Mary Helen, Verdie Kay, and Joy; and to my uncle, Guy Walton."

Dwight's third album Buenas Noches from a Lonely Room (1988) featured two number one singles. The first, "Streets of Bakersfield," was a duet with his idol Buck Owens. The second single, "I Sang Dixie," tells the story of the song's narrator meeting a man from the southern United States dying on a Los Angeles street. Dwight said that he wrote the song after him and his brother, during a visit to Los Angeles, witnessed some "stuff" in Hollywood that disturbed them both.

Dwight continued to release albums and singles for Reprise Records (Warner Brothers) for all of the 1990s and part of the 2000s. His albums, during this time, included This Time (1993), Dwight Live (1995), Come on Christmas (1997), and A Long Way Home (1998). In 2003, Dwight released the album Population Me on the label Koch-Audium. Dwight then signed with New West Records and released Blame the Vain (2005) and the tribute album Dwight Sings Buck (2007).

In 2014, Dwight returned to Warner Brothers records where he released 3 Pears. The album included collaborations with Kid Rock, Beck, and Ashley Monroe and was one of his most critically acclaimed albums. Dwight's next album, Second Hand Heart, was released in 2015.

Dwight began his acting career in 1991 with a guest appearance as a stuntman/country singer on the TV show *P.S I. Luv U*. He has since appeared in both dramatic and comedic films. Dwight is best known for his critically acclaimed performance as an ill-tempered abusive boyfriend in *Slingblade* (1996). His other roles include a psychopathic killer in *Panic Room* (2002), a cameo in *Wedding Crashers* (2005), and Pastor Phil in *Four Christmases* (2010). Dwight co-wrote, starred in, and wrote the soundtrack for the movie *South of Heaven, West of Hell* (2000) which starred Vince Vaughn. In 2014, Dwight starred in seven episodes of the second season of Stephen King's *Under the Dome*. He played Lyle Chumley who ran the barbershop in Chester's Mill.

Dwight has won numerous awards and honors including an ACM for New Male Vocalist of the Year, an ACM Cliffie Stone Pioneer Award, a Grammy for Best New Male Vocalist, and a Grammy for Best Musical Collaboration with Vocals. On June 5, 2003, he received a star on the Hollywood Walk of Fame.

In 2008, Dwight was inducted into the Kentucky Music Hall of Fame. During his acceptance speech, he stated that his induction "is an honor that will eclipse I think anything in my life." Dwight concluded his speech by saying, "I remember on all those journeys which we moved out and went to Ohio, as I said earlier that everything that I was going to be about and I am about till this point in my life comes from southeastern Kentucky."

Dwight holds the record for the most frequent musical guest on The Tonight Show and is the co-founder of Bakersfield Biscuits which sells frozen food at retailers such as Kroger and Walgreens. He continues to record albums and tour. Dwight is a voracious reader who stated in the Smiley interview, "I love knowledge. I think that we come to a greater understanding of the world we live in and ourselves, you know through reading."

McVeigh, Kentucky

Located in Pike County, McVeigh, Kentucky is an unincorporated community and coal town. The community had a post office until it closed in 2004.

Molly O'Day

Molly O'Day was born Lois LaVerne Williamson on July 9, 1923. Her parents, Joseph and Hester Williamson, raised Molly and her siblings on a farm in McVeigh, Kentucky. Her father worked as a coalminer. As a child, Molly listened to and was fascinated by cowgirl singers Patsy Montana, Lulu Belle Wiseman, Texas Ruby Owens, and Lily May Ledford.

Molly began practicing and singing with her brothers; Joe "Duke" on banjo and Cecil "Skeets" on fiddle. The three started playing at local dances and, in 1939, Skeets was hired to perform in the WCHS (Charleston, West Virginia) radio band, Ervin Staggs and his Radio Ramblers. The same year, Molly joined the band as a vocalist under the name Mountain Fern.

The next year was a busy year. Molly worked with banjoist Murphy McClees. Then, she and brothers moved to Williamson, West Virginia to perform at a local radio station. Finally, they moved to Beckley, West Virginia to join the Happy Valley Boys led by Johnnie Bailes. The band didn't make much of a profit so it disintegrated in the fall of 1940.

The same year, Molly applied for and became a vocalist with Lynn Davis and his Forty-Niners who had performed on WHIS in Bluefield, West Virginia for the past four years. Molly was now performing under the pseudonym Dixie Lee Williamson. In addition to being a vocalist, Molly played guitar and a 5-string banjo. On April 5, 1941, Molly married Lynn Davis.

The Forty-Niners performed at several locations in the southwest including a show in Birmingham, Alabama with Hank Williams Sr. In 1945, Lynn decided to change the name of the band to the Cumberland Mountain Folks. The following year, the band became a mainstay in Louisville, Kentucky and Molly changed her performing name to Molly O'Day due to the fact that there was a singer named Dixie Lee. Molly and Lynn's duets were popular but it was Molly's solo performances that audiences most responded to.

In the mid-1940s, Molly began performing songs written by Hank Williams Sr. who introduced her to her most beloved song, "Tramp on the Street," written by Grady Cole. Upon hearing Molly's rendition of the song, Fred Rose, head of Acuff-Rose, arranged a Columbia Records recording contract for Molly in 1946. In December, Molly O'Day and The Cumberland Mountain Folks made their first recording in Chicago, Illinois which featured eight tracks including "Tramp on the Street." Molly was backed on the album by Lynn, Skeets, dobro player George "Speedy" Krise, and bluegrass legend and bassist Mac Wiseman.

The recording boosted Molly's popularity but she began having trouble coping with success. As a result, Molly and Lynn spent much of 1947 away from the spotlight but did return to the studio in December for Molly to record the crowd pleaser "Matthew Twenty-Four." Molly, along with Lynn, spent the next several years on the road and started performing religious material almost exclusively.

In April 1949 at a recording session in Nashville, Tennessee, Molly recorded a number of songs including "Teardrops Falling in the Snow," "Poor Ellen Smith," and "On the Evening Train" which was written by Hank Williams Sr. The resulting album was chosen for the Smithsonian Collection and "Teardrops Falling In The Snow" was billed in the Smithsonian Manual as "a recording which unites one of the greatest country singers with one of the most compelling songs about the tragedy of war."

In the latter half of 1949, Molly took some time off from music, for personal reasons, but was able to return to recording in 1950 and 1951. However, she largely turned away from show business and focused on performing in churches. In 1952, Molly retired at age twenty-nine.

In 1954, Lynn became a minister and he and Molly began preaching in coal mining communities throughout West Virginia. The pair attended a church in Huntington, West Virginia and ran a record shop in Williamson, West Virginia, in the coal fields near the Kentucky border.

In the 1960s, Molly recorded for a few labels including GRS Records where the focus was on recording "real country" and REM which was based in Lexington, Kentucky. Despite these recording sessions, Molly's preference was to sing in churches and to do evangelical work. Both the Smithsonian Institute and Ralph Stanley tried to convince Molly to go back onstage but were unsuccessful. In 1973, Molly and Lynn started a daily gospel program on a Christian radio station in Huntington, West Virginia.

Molly died on December 5, 1987 in Huntington at the age of sixty-four. She is remembered as a pioneering vocalist whose performances helped redefine the role of the female country solo artist. Former music critic, for The New York Times, Robert Shelton referred to Molly as "one of the greatest, if not the greatest, women singers in country music." Bluegrass banjo player Earl Scruggs recalled that he was once beat by Molly in a Kentucky banjo-picking contest and that he had been awed by her banjo playing and singing. Dolly Parton said that Molly's singing had profoundly influenced her. Despite her success and recognition, Molly refused honors and insisted that her career had no impact on modern country music.

Virgie, Kentucky

Virgie, Kentucky is located in Pike County. On April 3, 1890, the post office was established as Clintwood. The postmaster was James M. Damron. It was renamed Virgie after the daughter of W.O.B. Ratliff, a local resident, lawyer, and lumber dealer in Pikeville.

Josh Osborne

Josh Shaun Osborne was born in 1980 and raised in Virgie, Kentucky by his parents Stanley and Geraldine Osborne. Growing up, Josh developed a deep love of country music, especially for Keith Whitley and Dwight Yoakam, and played in various bands. Josh feels that the presence of the Country Music Highway gives young musicians the idea that a career in music is possible. In an interview with Rich Copley for the Lexington Herald Leader, Josh described his musical appreciation of his fellow members of the highway, "I pretty much love everybody on Country Music Highway because they were all played on the radio when I was a kid. I had a love for country music before I even knew what country music was."

Josh performed his first show at age three. Around age thirteen, he began writing songs after receiving encouragement from his father. In the Copley interview, Josh described his start with songwriting, "My dad said, 'If you like music so much, you know the great ones write their own music' and he turned me on to The Beatles. So I listened to this song "Norwegian Wood" and that made me want to be a songwriter. Something clicked in my brain with how the words fell together with the melody. I like singing music and playing music but I just found this passion for writing."

As a teenager, Josh began making trips to Nashville, Tennessee where he met a couple of staff writers who saw him play at open mic nights and encouraged him. In an interview with Liv Carter, Josh described these early trips, "My parents were a huge influence on my love of music and my career. They started bringing me to Nashville when I was fifteen. I had been writing songs for about a year and then came to Nashville and started co-writing with people at a young age. It was like being in school, you know. There was a writer named Terry Vonderheide who unfortunately just passed away. He was the first person I ever co-wrote a song with here and I learned a lot from him. I quickly began to love co-writing, more than writing alone. I love the light bulb moments where you're talking to someone and they say something different than you would or they interpret something in a different way. I really began to love that. That was kind of a big moment for me. I don't write a lot by myself and when I do nine times out of ten it becomes an idea that I take to someone else. I learned more from the co-writing that I could ever have understood on my own."

After graduating from Shelby Valley High School (Pikeville, Kentucky), in 1998, Josh moved to Nashville. In an interview with Bill Conger for Songwriter Universe, Josh described the goals he had and how they changed, "When I first moved to Nashville, I think I came here more with the intent of writing and singing my own songs, mostly because I didn't know that writing songs was an option, to come here and be a full-time behind-the-scenes songwriter. Once I moved here and started writing songs with people, I really fell in love with that part of it. I never had that same kind of love for doing the singing part of it. I think of myself more as a vehicle for the song. I want it to be more about the song than me, so I like doing writer's nights and playing songs for people. It's more because I want them to notice the songs and not me." At age eighteen, Josh signed his first publishing deal with Chappell Music.

Around 2007, Josh decided to change his songwriting approach during a writing session with long-time songwriting partner Trevor Rosen. Around this time, Josh met fellow songwriter Shane McAnally. He described these experiences in the Conger interview, "Trevor came in to write one day and said, 'What do you want to write today?' I said, 'They don't cut anything we write anyway. Let's just write something we like and something that when we leave the room, I want to get into my car and listen to it, or I want to be excited to play it for people as opposed to trying chase a cut or chase what's on the radio.' From that moment, my brain started to work differently and I started to write songs in a different way. That was a big turning point for me."

He continued, "[Shane] didn't have a publishing deal. We met at the right time where we were both right on the cusp of things starting to happen. He was another big thing for me. For some reason at that point, I started to feel like success was attainable. You've got a lot of years where you write songs and you honestly feel like I'm never going to get a song recorded. That day with Trevor and meeting Shane–those were the two big moments where all of a sudden I thought I'm going to do this. It's going to work out."

In 2010, Josh switched publishing companies and signed with Black River Entertainment. The following year, Josh achieved success when he had his first song cut, "Neon" by Chris Young. Josh's first number one song was Kenny Chesney's "Come Over." The song was released in 2012 and spent two weeks on top of the Billboard Country Airplay charts. In the Copley interview, Josh described his feelings, "There was a relief, like, 'I'm not crazy. I can do this'."

One of Josh's biggest hits to date is Kasey Musgrave's "Merry Go 'Round" which he co-wrote with Kasey and Shane. The song was released in 2012, reached the top ten on Billboard Country Airplay charts, sold ten million copies, achieved platinum status, and won a Grammy Award for Best Country Song of the Year in recognition of the songwriters. The trio wrote the song during a writers retreat at Crawford Ranch in Strawn, Texas where the focus was writing songs for Kasey's upcoming album.

Before heading to the retreat, Josh attended a 4th of July picnic at Shane's mother's house in Mineral Wells, Texas. In the Copley interview, Josh described the song's origins, "Someone [at the picnic] noticed that one of the neighbors had a lot of traffic at their house, a lot of cars there, and they said, 'What are they doing?' Shane's mom said, 'I don't know what they're doing. They're selling Mary Kay or Mary Jane or something.' I said to Shane, 'There's a song in that, there's a great small-town song in that.' He's from a small town in Texas, I'm from a small town- Virgie, Kentucky is about as small as it gets, and Kacey's from a small town in Texas. So when we got together, we started talking about that line and living in a small town and how everybody knows everybody and everybody kind of knows what's going on."

During the Conger interview, Josh explained his personal feelings about the lyrics, "I grew up in a coal-mining town, so the whole line about "counting little boxes in a row" for me, that was the little coal-mining houses that they built on a side of a mountain. That song was such a representation for me from my heart of where I grew up."

In 2015, Josh joined Shane's company SMACK Songs as a partner and songwriter. The label represents Shane, Matthew Ramsey, and Trevor Rosen.

Josh has had radio singles released by a variety of artists including "We Are Tonight" by Billy Currington, "Real Life" by Jake Owen, "Top of the World" by Tim McGraw, "John Cougar, John Deere, John 3:16" by Keith Urban, "Chainsaw" by The Band Perry, "Sangria" by Blake Shelton, and "Vice" by Miranda Lambert. In addition, he has had songs recorded by Joe Nichols, Easton Corbin, Rodney Adkins, and Luke Bryan. Several of Josh's songs have been awarded Gold and Platinum status.

In addition to his Grammy award, he won Song of the Year at the 2013 MusicRow Awards for "Merry Go 'Round," Songwriter of the Year at the 2015 ASCAP Country Awards for the song "Take Your Time" recorded by Sam Hunt, two ASCAP Awards for the "Most Performed Songs of the Year," the NSAI Award for "Song I Wish I Had Written," and Music Row Magazine's "Song of the Year." Jason was introduced into Pike County School's Hall of Fame for his musical talent and success.

On June 11, 2014, Josh's name was added to the Country Music Highway in a ceremony held in Pike County. About the honor, Josh said, "Growing up on Country Music Highway, knowing how much all those artists have influenced and inspired me, and now to think that I am even a small part of that heritage means the world to me. I honestly don't think any honor could mean more to me."

Josh enjoys writing music and has no desire to have a career as a performer. In the Copley interview, he stated, "I prefer writing the songs and letting someone else take them on tour while I sit at home and watch Kentucky basketball." He currently lives in Nashville with his wife Toni.

Dorton, Kentucky

Located in southern Pike County, Dorton, Kentucky is an unincorporated community and coal town. The community was named after William P. Dorton. The post office was established on July 2, 1872 and the first postmaster was John Bumgardner.

Marlow Tackett

Marlow Tackett was born on February 28, 1944 in Dorton, Kentucky to his parents Toy and Frona Vanover Tackett. His parents raised him and his siblings in a small house on a hillside farm. Toy worked as a cutting machine operator at two different coal mines. In an interview with Ked Sanders for the Letcher County Community News-Press, Marlow discussed his childhood, "I was reared in a family of eighteen kids and we never had a lot of worldly goods. Even though my dad worked two jobs, life was still tough."

All of the family shared responsibility, they farmed and kept livestock. Marlow was responsible for bringing the cow home and described this during in an interview with Ken Sanders and Patsy Tackett for the Mountain Eagle, "I had this pup named Elvis because at that time I idolized Elvis Presley's music. Someone had set the pup out on the side of the road and he followed me home. I took Elvis to the pasture with me to help me bring home the cow. After a few trips, Elvis knew how to herd the cow himself. The cow would hide in the edge of the woods and try to avoid Elvis. Sooner or later the cow would move and the cowbell around her neck would tinkle and Elvis would take off like greased lighting to bring her in. Because I didn't have to get the cow anymore I stayed at the bottom of the hill and strummed on the barbed wire fence and sang Elvis Presley's songs literally till the cow came home. Even on a cold, gray, wintery evening with dusk coming fast I stayed warm as I dreamed of some day getting a guitar and becoming a rock and roll singer like Elvis Presley. When I wasn't strumming on the barbed wire fence, I was beating on a broom, a can or anything trying to make music.

When Marlow was around nine years old, he entered and won first place at a talent contest at Dorton Elementary School. In the Mountain Eagle article, Marlow recalled the experience, "My older sister, Audrey, took Maybelline and painted me some sideburns. Then she took some white shoe polish and blue cake coloring and painted my shoes blue. I didn't have a guitar but oh! how I wanted one. I tried to imitate Elvis's body gyrations by pretending that I was itching all over and didn't have enough hands to scratch. I sang "Blue Suede Shoes" and won $2.50 and a box of Milky Way candy bars."

He continued by telling how he won the countywide 4-H talent contest the same year, "The winner was to get to perform at the Liberty Theater in Pikeville [Kentucky]. Our family didn't have a car so my parents didn't get to go see me perform. I didn't have any dress clothes so Reo Johns, a schoolteacher at Dorton, bought me a pair of pants, shirt, and jacket and took me to Pikeville to perform."

In the Mountain Eagle interview, Marlow remembered the experience of getting his first guitar, "One night my dad woke me at 1:30 in the morning when he got home from work. He got me out of bed and took me into the kitchen. There set the prettiest thing I ever laid two eyes on in my life. He had bought me a Montgomery Ward Harmony guitar at Brack Little's store in the head of Caney Creek. He taught me a few basic chords then I learned the rest on my own. My career was launched. Dad always encouraged me. When company would come Dad would say 'Git your guitar, Bub, and sing for these folks'."

Marlow loved his guitar so much that he wanted it with him all the time. He chose to play it while the other children played ball. Marlow was warned by the principal that he had to stop playing his guitar on the school bus or he wouldn't be allowed to ride it anymore. Starting that day, Marlow no longer rode the bus and either walked or hitched a ride to school.

When Marlow was sixteen years old, his father got sick and was unable to work like he had before. Marlow knew the family was struggling financially so he figured if he left home and got a job, there would be one less mouth to feed. Also, he was getting anxious to follow his dream of being a professional singer. In the Mountain Eagle interview, he discussed the move, his experiences, and his eventual return to Kentucky, "I went to Fort Wayne, Indiana, where my older brother, Obie, lived. I didn't even look for a job doing manual labor. I got gigs singing at various theaters, schools, bar rooms, or any place I could. I was actually making a living doing what I wanted to do. I continued honing my skills then I auditioned at the Brooklyn Inn Theater and Night Club. I sang there three nights a week for a year. One of the people who came to my show often was the owner of the Piano Club in downtown Fort Wayne. He said, 'I don't know what you are making here but I will pay you double if you will come and work for me.' I took the job and was living my dream. I performed all over the country, then went to Nashville, Tennessee and played some gigs there. After three and a half years, I had seen enough of the bright lights of the cities and I was ready to come home to Kentucky."

After returning home, Marlow would perform on the bed of a flatbed truck. Word began to spread about his talent and a growing number of people came to see him perform. When it got close to winter, Marlow, knowing he would need an indoor location, bought some land and built a facility out of rough sawmill lumber and called it The Country Corral. The venue had a small stage, wooden benches, and a sawdust covered floor.

The Country Corral was popular among patrons and outgrew the building which led to Marlow renting several locations before finding a permanent building in Pikeville. In 1975, he opened Marlow's Country Palace which he operated successfully for thirty years. Marlow performed shows four days a week in addition to bringing a variety of artists to the venue including George Jones and Gary Stewart.

In 1977, Marlow was performing at a show in Lexington, Kentucky that was broadcast live nationwide to 120 stations. Ralph Emory, the emcee for the show, invited Marlow to be on his early morning radio show that was broadcast throughout the southeastern United States. Next, Ralph booked Marlow on his TV show *Pop Goes the Country* which led to him appearing on the *Porter Waggoner Show*. This national exposure led to Marlow releasing several singles and eventually signing a three year contract with RCA Records in 1982.

Before partnering with RCA, Marlow recorded the singles "Mellow Me Down" and "Would You Know Love" in 1979 with NSP. During his time at RCA, he recorded and released several singles including "Ever-Lovin' Woman" (1982), "634-5789" (1982), "I Know My Way By Heart" (1983), and "I Spent The Night In The Heart of Texas" (1983). Additionally, Marlow appeared on the Grand Ole Opry three times.

Marlow decided not to renew his contract with RCA and focused on running Marlow's Country Palace and his other successful businesses. In the Mountain Eagle interview, Marlow reflected about his decision, "Sometimes I look back and wonder if that was the right decision. Sometimes people just have to follow their heart. Not only was the best money here at home but my heart was here in the mountains with people I love."

In addition to his Country Palace performances, Marlow was willing to perform at churches, schools, political gatherings, and benefits. Marlow had an experience in 1976 that greatly shaped his future in regards to charitable contributions. He described this experience in the Letcher County Community News-Press interview, "I have literally done thousands of benefit shows and have never charged for them. That has always been my way of giving back to the people who made me successful. It was as a result of one of those benefit shows in 1976, that a little girl sent me a letter requesting some help in making a nice Christmas for her family."

When Marlow and his band arrived at the family's house they found that there was no electric, water, or presents and the little girl and her four brothers were in tattered clothing. Marlow helped this family have a good Christmas but also realized that there must be more children in need which led to him hosting an annual Christmas party for families in need starting in 1977.

In the Letcher County Community News Press interview, Marlow commented, "That Christmas was as rewarding for me as it was for her [the little girl] and her family." The first year, 450 families were served with the number growing in subsequent years. Marlow would partner with businesses, churches, and civic organizations when organizing the parties. Recipients received toys, clothes, furniture, and other items. As a result of Marlow's generosity, he earned the nickname "Mountain Santa."

In addition to the Christmas parties, Marlow would do a tour of nursing homes, rest homes, and health care centers in Pike, Floyd, Letcher, Martin, Magoffin, and Johnson Counties. He was willing to help victims of house fires, flood victims, raise money for individuals who were sick and/or destitute, and would collect food and clothing for needy children in Pike County schools. Due to his work with the school system, Marlow was designated as honorary Pike County school superintendant.

After Marlow's Country Palace closed, Marlow performed at various locations throughout the Pike County area and surrounding states. During his career, Marlow recorded a minimum of ten albums including a gospel album A New Set of Wings. He wrote ten of the twelve songs on the album.

Marlow passed away on May 10, 2014 at seventy years old in Elizabethtown, Tennessee. He is buried at Tackett Cemetery in Dorton. Marlow is remembered as an artist and humanitarian who enjoyed life. He had a passion for trading things like cars and horses. Marlow is survived by six sons and five daughters.

Elkhorn City, Kentucky

Elkhorn City, Kentucky in Pike County is located at the foothills of the Appalachian Mountains. The city has a population of 982 according to the 2010 census.

In 1767 or 1768, Daniel Boone, on a hunting trip, took his first steps in what is now Kentucky near present-day Elkhorn City. The city was settled by William Ramey of North Carolina around 1810. The original name was Elkhorn after an elk's horn that was found on the banks of the nearby creek. The town had to be renamed due to the fact that there was an "Elk Horn" in Taylor County.

On October 16, 1882, the post office was renamed Praise for the tent colony "Camp Praise-the-Lord" that was established by evangelist George O. Barnes for a revival held in August 1881. In 1907, a C&O Railroad station was established in Praise and named Elkhorn City. On November 4, 1912, Elkhorn City was incorporated as a city but the local post office was not renamed Elkhorn City until September 1, 1952 after local pressure for a uniform name.

Patty Loveless

Patty Loveless was born Patricia Lee Ramey on January 4, 1957. Her parents, John and Naomie Ramey, had seven children and Patty was the youngest girl. Her cousin, Dicie, also lived with the family.

John worked in the coal mines and the family lived in Elkhorn City, Kentucky. The family loved music and would listen to the Grand Ole Opry on Friday and Saturday nights using a radio propped up in the kitchen window. At age three, Patty began singing along with the songs while her mother mopped the floors. When singing for company, Patty would go to another room since she was too shy to look at her audience. Patty saw her first live show when her father took her to see Flatt & Scruggs and the Foggy Mountain Boys perform on top of the concession stand during an intermission at the local Polly Ann drive-in theater.

In 1969, the Ramey family moved to Louisville, Kentucky so John, who was suffering from "Black Lung Disease," could receive medical care. Patty was having a hard time adjusting at her new school so John bought her a guitar and sent her to lessons. Patty's parents were very protective of her and she wasn't allowed to go anywhere in Louisville by herself. Her brother, Michael, would chaperone her on dates.

At age twelve, Patty, her mother, and siblings visited her older brother, Wayne, who was in the army. During the visit in Fort Knox, Tennessee, a country band was playing so Patty's mother informed the guitar player that she had a daughter that sang. Since they were short a female singer, they invited Patty's sister, Dottie, to join them on stage. Patty remembers how beautiful Dottie looked in a brown suit that matched her hair. It was at that time that Patty decided she wanted to be a singer.

Dottie and her brother, Roger, were a duo that performed at locations around town. After getting married, Dottie quit the duo and Roger pushed for Patty to replace her. Her first performance onstage was at a jamboree in Louisville. She was so terrified that she developed a rash but, at the same time, instantly loved it. She earned five dollars for doing the show; it was the first money she had ever earned. Local DJ and friend Danny King named the duo the "Singin' Swingin' Rameys" and they began performing around Louisville.

In 1970, Roger moved to Nashville and became a producer on the *Porter Waggoner Show*. When Patty was fourteen years old, she went with Roger to Porter's office where she performed some of her original music. This performance included "Sound of Loneliness," a song Patty had wrote for her father.

Porter encouraged Patty to finish school but did agree to help her and invited her to travel with him and Dolly Parton on weekends and in the summer. Dolly gave Patty advice on a variety of topics ranging from songwriting to makeup. The same year, she was able to visit the Opry as Porter and Dolly's guest.

In 1973, Bill Anderson, Connie Smith, the Wilburn Brothers, and Jean Shepherd were scheduled to appear at a traveling Grand Ole Opry Show in Louisville Gardens. Shepherd had to cancel due to being caught in a flood and the Ramey kids were asked to fill in for her. They performed for about fifteen minutes.

Doyle Wilburn, of the Wilburn Brothers, saw their performance and asked Patty, age sixteen, if she'd ever performed professionally. She explained that she'd been working and traveling with Porter Waggoner and Dolly Parton. Doyle asked if she would be interested in working with the band. Patty began traveling with the Wilburn Brothers on weekends and in the summer. Her parents insisted that the Wilburns look out for her while she was on the road.

Since he knew Patty was a talented songwriter, Doyle held a publishing contract on her at his songwriting agency Sure-Fire Music. He was slowly grooming her to replace their lead female singer, Loretta Lynn (whom is a distant cousin to Patty). During the summer, when the group wasn't touring, Patty worked at Doyle's different businesses in Nashville which included waiting tables and clerking at Music Mart USA.

In 1975, Patty graduated from Fairdale High School in Louisville and became the Wilburn Brother's lead female singer. Patty met the band's new drummer, Terry Lovelace, who reminded her of guys from Pikeville, Kentucky. The two formed a relationship that they kept secret for a while.

Patty was beginning to feel suffocated traveling with the Wilburns so both her and Terry quit the band. On Patty's nineteenth birthday, the couple moved to King's Mountain, North Carolina where Terry was from. In early 1976, they got married and began performing around the King's Mountain area. Patty did covers of late 70s rock songs including Linda Ronstadt and Bonnie Raitt tunes mixed with an occasional country song. When Patty wasn't performing, she would waitress in her mother-in-law's restaurant.

In April 1985, Patty knew that her marriage was over but decided to keep a version of her married name by changing Lovelace to Loveless. Roger helped his sister get back to Nashville to cut a five-song demo tape. Roger used the demo to try and get his sister a recording contract. After a month of rejections, Roger took the tape to MCA Nashville and bluffed his way past the receptionist for Tony

Brown, head of Artist and Repertoire, by pretending to be someone else.

Roger told Brown he had 'the best girl singer to ever come to Nashville.' Brown gave him thirty seconds to sell him on Patty so Roger played the song "I Did," which Patty had wrote as a teenager. Brown ended up listening to the other four songs and then played it for MCA President Jimmy Bowen who offered her a short-term recording contract. As a result, Patty started working with producer Emory Gordy Jr.

In 1986, Patty was offered an album deal and recorded her self-titled album. In 1988, Patty had her first number one single "Timber, I'm Falling in Love" and was inducted into the Grand Ole Opry. The following year, she married Emory. Patty released four more albums with MCA and continued to tour as an opening act for artists such as George Strait and George Jones.

In 1992, Patty left MCA and signed a contract with Sony under their Epic label. During her recording sessions, Gordy noticed that Patty's voice wasn't as strong. Patty had a leaking vessel on her vocal chords that required her to have corrective surgery. As a result, she had to cancel her tour and was unable to speak or sing for nine weeks.

On January 4, 1993, Patty re-entered the music world and performed at the Grand Ole Opry. Upon returning to the studio, her voice was more powerful than before so all the previous album recordings were scrapped and redone. In April 1993, she released her first album for Epic, <u>Only Feel What I Feel</u>. Her first single from the album, "Blame It on Your Heart," went to number one. Her follow-up album, <u>When Angels Fly</u>, won the CMA Album of the Year and produced four top ten singles.

In 2001, Patty, inspired by the Appalachian music she heard as a child, released the bluegrass album <u>Mountain Soul</u>. Patty and Emory both considered the project, which was dedicated to her parents, to be a labor of love. Patty released a Christmas album, <u>Bluegrass and White Snow</u>, in 2002 and continued to record for Epic until 2005.

In 2006 and 2007, Patty took a sabbatical from touring and enjoyed some time at home. In 2007, she was a judge for the sixth annual Independent Music Awards. She has appeared on tracks with George Strait and Jimmy Wayne.

Patty has won three CMAs including one with George Strait in 1988 for Vocal Event of the Year: "You Don't Seem to Miss Me." Additionally, she has won two ACMs for Female Vocalist of the Year (1995/1996) and two Grammy Awards for Best Country Collaboration with Vocals: "Same Old Train" (1998) and Best Bluegrass Album: Mountain Soul II (2011). Patty was inducted into the Kentucky Music Hall of Fame in 2011.

Patty no longer performs on a regular basis but does make an annual appearance at the Grand Ole Opry and attends an annual country music cruise. In 2001, Patty and Emory moved from Nashville to a countryside home near Dallas, Georgia to be near Emory's family. Patty, who has two stepdaughters, says there is a sense of peace in waking up and knowing where you are after years of living out of a suitcase. In an interview with Tom Roland, she described her new house, "This is my final home. I've told everybody I'm gonna live here, die here, and come back and haunt the place." She enjoys taking walks, hiking the hills near her property, and growing a garden.

Pikeville, Kentucky

Located in Pike County, the city of Pikeville, Kentucky has 6,903 residents (2010 U.S. census) and is the county seat. On March 25, 1822, state officials make the decision to build a new county seat a mile and a half below the mouth of the Russell Fork River and name it "Liberty." However, public disapproval of this site led officials to a new decision on December 24, 1823. The county seat was to be established on land donated by Elijah Adkins, a local farmer. In 1824, the settlement was established and named Pike after the county. In 1829, the name was changed to Piketon and was incorporated in 1848. In 1850, it was changed again to the present name of Pikeville.

Pikeville played host to part of the Hatfield-McCoy feud. The feud, which lasted from 1863-1891, was between the Hatfield family of West Virginia and the McCoy family of Kentucky.

Pikeville had been rapidly growing since the 1990s and is home to the University of Pikeville (previously known as Pikeville College). In 1997, the University opened the Kentucky College of Osteopathic Medicine. In October 2005, the 7,000 seat, multi-purpose Eastern Kentucky Exposition Center opened downtown.

McCarr, Kentucky

McCarr, Kentucky is an unincorporated community and coal town located in Pike County. As of July 1, 2016, McCarr had a population of 182 residents.

Junior Hager and the Melody Drifters

Junior Hager and The Melody Drifters was a country/western band. The band was made up of McCarr, Kentucky native Wayne Edwards and Pikeville, Kentucky natives Bill Abernathy, Eugene Prewitt, and Earl Duty. Wayne chose the stage name Junior Hager because his foster parents' last name was Hager.

In the 1940s, the band was formed in Pikeville. Junior played guitar, sang lead, and wrote songs, Joe Dado played steel guitar (later replaced by Bill Abernathy), Eugene played acoustic guitar, and Earl played bass. Junior Hager and The Melody Drifters played throughout Eastern Kentucky in the 1950s and 60s.

The band began their broadcast career at WLSI-AM in Pikeville. They had the opportunity to perform on the Grand Ole Opry. In June 2010, Junior Hager and The Melody Drifters were added to the Country Music Highway. Junior and Joe attended the event.

Jenkins, Kentucky

Jenkins, a city in Letcher County Kentucky, has a population of 2,203 according to the 2010 census. In the fall of 1911, the Northern Coal and Coke Company sold the current location of Jenkins to the Consolidation Coal Company as part of 100,000 acre tract of land spanning three counties (Floyd, Letcher, and Pike). After the sale was final, plans were made to extend the Lexington and Eastern Railroad from two Kentucky towns, Jackson and McRoberts. Included in these plans was the establishment of the town of Jenkins to be named after George C. Jenkins, one of the directors for the Consolidation Coal Company.

Hundreds of homes and other structures including nine sawmills and two brickyards were built out of need. To further the development of the town, a temporary narrow-gauge railroad was built to carry supplies over Pine Mountain (a ridge in the Appalachian Mountains) from Glamorgan, Virginia.

The government of Jenkins was established when the business and land were put up for sale. Finally, Jenkins was incorporated on January 9, 1912. The town is best known as being the birthplace of the two Garys: country music star Gary Stewart and U-2 spy plane pilot Francis Gary Powers.

Gary Stewart

Gary Ronnie Stewart, named after actor Gary Cooper, was born May 28, 1944 in Jenkins, Kentucky. His parents, George and Georgia Stewart, had eleven children all of whom have first names that start with the letter "G." George, a coal miner, was injured while working and, as a result, the family moved to Fort Pierce, Florida, in 1959, when Gary was twelve years old.

After the move, Gary learned to play piano and guitar and started to write songs. Shannon Stewart, Gary's daughter, described her father's beginning in music, "He mowed lawns to get money for a guitar and he taught himself how to play guitar. It was his mother's birthday and he was eighteen years old, he rented some kind of studio time to lay down this song he wrote "I Love You Truly." And that was the first song he ever put down and it was for his mother's birthday."

As a teenager, he began touring with local bands including playing bass with the rock group The Amps. Gary, who was drawn to both country and rock and roll, formed his own band The Tomcats. At age seventeen, he started working full-time at an airplane factory and, then at night, playing music at clubs. In 1962, Gary married Mary Lou Taylor who was three years older than him.

Gary met singer Mel Tillis while working at the Wagon Wheel, a honky-tonk in Okeechobee, Florida. Mel advised him to go to Nashville, Tennessee and pitch his songs. Gary and his family moved to Nashville for him to pursue a musical career.

During this time, he played piano in Charley Pride's band The Pridesman and appeared on his live <u>In Person</u> album. During an interview on Nashville Now, Gary spoke about this experience, "I was playing piano for Charley Pride. Charley really helped me. I played piano for him for a couple of years."

In 1964, Gary recorded a few songs for the small label Cory before signing with KAPP in 1968. He eventually grew tired of Nashville and decided to move back to Florida. After the move, Gary started developing a new, gritty sound that reflected his recent interest in the Southern rockers the Allman Brothers, whom he later became friends with.

Gary began co-writing songs with Bill Eldridge, a former member of the Tomcats and local policeman. The pair wrote Grand Ole Opry star Stonewall Jackson's 1965 hit "Poor Red Georgia Dirt." They also wrote songs for artists including Cal Smith ("You Can't Housebreak a Tomcat" and "It Takes Me All Night Long"), Nat Stuckey ("Sweet Thing and Cisco"), and Billy Walker who had an affinity for their work ("She Goes Walking Through My Mind," "Traces of a Woman," and "It's Time to Love Her").

In the late 1960s, Gary pitched songs to Jerry Bradley who soon accepted a prominent position at RCA records. Bradley introduced Gary to producer Roy Dea. In 1973, Gary moved back to Nashville and recorded a version of Wayne Carson's "Drinkin' Song" which wasn't successful at the time. Next, he released a cover of Allman Brothers' "Ramblin' Man" which achieved some airplay. The success of the song prompted RCA to re-release "Drinkin' Thing" in 1974 which became a top ten hit.

Gary's album Out of Hand (1975) reached number six on the Country Album charts. In addition to "Drinkin' Thing," the album featured the title cut "Out of Hand" which reached number four and the single "She's Actin' Single (I'm Drinking Doubles)" which hit number one on the country charts. The album has become one of the most critically acclaimed albums of the 1970s. Praise for the album includes critic Robert Christgau saying the album "was the best country LP I've heard in years," Rolling Stone magazine stating, "With practitioners like Stewart around, honky-tonk and rockabilly may not be dead yet," and critic Bill Malone saying Out of Hand is "one of the greatest honky-tonk country albums ever recorded." Later the same year, MCA re-released some of Gary's KAPP material including "You're Not The Woman You Used To Be."

Gary continued to perform at honky-tonks for the rest of the decade with his band the Honky Tonk Liberation Army and to record similar albums including Your Place or Mine (1977) which featured guest artists Rodney Crowell and Emmylou Harris. In 1980, he released his album Cactus and a Rose with featured artists Gregg Allan, Dickey Belts, Mike Lawler, and Bonnie Bramlett. Included on the album was the song "Harlan County Highway" which makes references to Kentucky including coal mines, Harlan County, and Louisville.

Gary recorded two duet albums with Dean Dillon. The song "Smokin' in the Rockies," wrote by Frank Dycus, Buddy Cannon, Gary Stewart, and Dean Dillon, was included on their 1983 album Those Were the Days. The song, which was released as a single, was then performed by country band Sawyer Brown on the television show *Star Search*. After winning the show, Sawyer Brown included it on their self-titled debut album.

Gary moved back to Florida and, in 1988, signed with the label High Tone. He released three albums in five years with singles including ones he wrote with his wife Mary Lou and Dean Dillon. Gary and Tanya Tucker wrote the song "There's a Tennessee Woman / Ben's Song" which was included on her album <u>Tennessee Woman</u> (1990). Additionally, many musicians traveled to Florida to write with Gary including Greg Allman, Willie Nelson, and Dickey Betts.

He continued to tour throughout the 1990s and would play at Billy Bob's Texas (Fort Worth, Texas) several times each year. In 2003, he released his first-ever live album, <u>Live at Billy Bob's Texas</u>. Gary had a large fan base in Texas and was named an honorary Texan. He would also play at fairs and benefits for people within the community who were in need.

Even though he moved at a young age, his daughter Shannon said that he always loved Kentucky and was thrilled that he got to serve as grand marshal of the Jenkins Homecoming Festival on August 29, 1998. The theme for the festival was Country Music Highway Take Me Home and recognized all of the U.S. 23 singers and songwriters from Eastern Kentucky. After the parade, Gary was shown the Country Music Highway sign that runs through the Jenkins area and recognizes him.

Later that night, he performed his first concert in his hometown. Jenkins resident Lorena Hill remembered the concert well and remarked, "He rocked this town, it was elbow to elbow." She remarked that there was nowhere on the street to park due to the large crowd and that the state police were called in an effort to control the parking situation. Ernestine Flint, local resident and organizer of the concert, stated that Gary's performance was "absolutely the largest crowd at Jenkins Days."

Gary passed away on December 16, 2003. He was preceded in death by his wife, Mary Lou, and his son, Joey. Gary is survived by his daughter, Shannon, his grandson, Joseph, whom was a special part of his life, and a great-grandson, Kash. Both Shannon and Joseph had traveled with Gary during his career.

Shannon described her father as "a very giving and caring individual. He would literally give you the shirt off his back you know. All of his fans, he always made time out for anybody and everybody. He never had a bad word to say about anybody. He was just very unique and he had such a kind heart." The one thing that she wants people to know about her father is "how much he loved everybody and how he didn't take a day for granted on all the respect he got from all his fans. And how much he loved music and how music was his life."

Gary and Mary Lou were both well thought of in their community of Fort Pierce. Following Gary's passing, his friends wrote letters to the editor of their community newspaper that spoke of both his talent and how much he would be missed. His friend, Mike Lewis, described Gary as "someone who was an awesome brother, son, father, performer, and spirit the like of who I'm quite sure I will not come across again."

Gary's music continues to be admired and enjoyed by fans and critics alike. Fellow singer Bob Dylan was so impressed with Gary's music that, while on tour in Florida, he drove out of his way to meet Gary confessing that he'd played Stewart's ode to marital malaise "Ten Years of This" over and over, the record 'casting a spell over him.'

Olive Hill, Kentucky

Located in Carter County, Olive Hill, Kentucky has a population of 1,599 according to the 2010 census. The Henderson Brothers established the city as a rural trading post during the first part of the 19th century. The official reason for the name "Olive Hill" is unknown but a popular theory is that Elias P. Davis named it for his friend Thomas Oliver.

The town was moved from the hillside location, a residential area known as Old Olive Hill, to the current "downhill" location in 1881. This location is in the Tygarts Creek valley and is where the Elizabethtown, Lexington, and Big Sandy Railroad had laid tracks. Olive Hill was incorporated as a city on March 24, 1884 and temporarily (February 9 to April 29, 1904) served as the county seat of the short-lived Beckham County.

Olive Hill and many other places were served by the Chesapeake and Ohio (C&O) Railway's Lexington Subdivision (ran from Ashland to Lexington). C&O merged into the Chessie System, which was later bought out by CSX Transportation, and eventually pulled up the railroad in the mid 1980s. The passenger depot and a caboose were both retained, restored, and are on display in town.

Tom T. Hall

Tom T. Hall was born on May 25, 1936 in a log cabin behind his grandfather's house on Tick Ridge in Olive Hill, Kentucky. He was named Thomas by his parents, Virgil Lee and Della Hall, and later decided to add the middle initial to make his name more distinctive. Tom, often known as "The Storyteller" to his fans, had five brothers and four sisters.

Tom began to write poetry at a young age so his progression to songwriting wasn't surprising. At age eight, Virgil, a bricklayer, gave Tom his first guitar. He began learning music and performing techniques from local musician Lonnie Easterly. Tom's fans know Lonnie as Clayton Delaney from the song "The Year Clayton Delaney Died." Lonnie's renaming came from the fact that he lived on Clayton Hill and his neighbors were the Delaney family. In an effort to keep the feel of what he was writing about, Tom kept everything on one hill and one neighborhood and, as a result, Lonnie became Clayton Delaney.

At age nine, Tom wrote his first song after overhearing his neighbors arguing with each other. The woman told her husband that she was going back to her mothers and left the house carrying a bag. Her husband responded, 'Well, haven't I been good to you?' Tom, using the line as inspiration, wrote the song "Haven't I Been Good To You" as a joke. He sang the song at the next family "backyard singing" where it was enjoyed by everyone. Instead of taking credit for the song, Tom said that he had heard the song on the radio.

By the time Tom was thirteen, he could sing and play all of the country favorites that were popular at the time. The same year, his mother passed away and Tom withdrew into books and music. Two years after that, his father was hurt in a hunting accident and could no longer work. In order to help out financially, Tom quit school and began working as a bundle boy at the local sewing factory.

While working at the factory, Tom formed his first band Kentucky Travelers. The band played bluegrass music and performed at the local schools. They also performed before movies for a traveling theater and at a radio station in nearby Morehead, Kentucky. Tom wrote a jingle for one of the station's sponsors, Polar Bear Flour. After Kentucky Travelers broke up, Tom took a job as a DJ at the same station.

In 1957, Tom enlisted in the Army and was stationed in Germany where he earned his high school diploma. While there, he would perform on the Armed Forces Radio Network and usually did original material that featured a comedic angle about army experiences. Tom was discharged, in 1961, after four years of service. After returning to the States, he enrolled in Roanoke College in Salem, Virginia as a journalism student and supported himself by working as a DJ.

In 1963, Tom received a phone call from Newskeys Publishing offering him a job as a professional songwriter. So, on January 1, 1964, he moved to Nashville, Tennessee with his guitar and $46. He met his future wife, Iris Dixie Dean better known as Miss Dixie, at the 1965 BMI Country Awards in Nashville. The pair got married in March 1968.

Tom wrote hundreds of songs on his typewriter, ranging from sad to funny. He didn't manage to write a "Tom T. Hall" song until he stopped making things up and started writing about things he knew. He did this by writing songs that were often biographical in nature. Tom wrote most songs by telling exactly what happened. It was then left up to the listener to figure out what the song was all about. In an effort to protect people's privacy, Tom would change the names of the people and the places.

He also stopped following the "rules" of song writing. For example, his 1969 top ten hit "Homecoming" doesn't even have the word homecoming in the lyrics. The song tells a story from the viewpoint of a son who comes home and tries to explain himself to his father. Tom explained the song in an interview with Craig Shelburne, "My father was a Baptist preacher, kind of what I'd call an ordinary person. But if you've got a son that wants to go off in the music business, it's pretty hard for them to grasp that. And when you come home after being out singing, they don't get exactly what you're doing. Everybody liked music, but nobody took it seriously and never thought of it as a profession. So when you come home, it's hard to explain what you're doing."

The change in Tom's songwriting occurred after country singer Stonewall Jackson asked Tom to write him a prison song for an album he was working on. After several failed attempts, Tom told Miss Dixie that he felt like a phony writing about prison since he'd never been there. She suggested he write about jail since he had spent time there. The result was the song "A Week in the County Jail." The song wasn't anything like Stonewall wanted so Tom decided not to present it but later recorded it himself.

In 1965, Johnny Wright had a number one hit with "Hello Vietnam," a song written by Tom. After the success of this song, Tom started receiving pressure from the music industry to become a performer. In 1967, Tom signed a recording contract with Mercury Records. His first single, "I Washed My Face in the Morning Dew," was a minor hit.

In 1968, Jeannie C. Riley released Tom's song "Harper Valley P.T.A." The song told the story of Mrs. Johnson, a widowed mother who had a teenage daughter who attended Harper Valley Junior High. Her daughter brought home a note from the Harper Valley P.T.A. describing how Mrs. Johnson was participating in "scandalous" behavior such as wearing her dresses way to high and running around with men. Mrs. Johnson responded by attending the next P.T.A. meeting wearing a mini-skirt. She then proceeded to detail several P.T.A. member's misbehavior and indiscretions.

Tom described the origins of the song, which was based on a true story, "There were ten kids in our family. We'd get up in the morning, and my mother and father would get bored with us running around, and we'd go terrorize the neighbors up and down this little road we lived on- after we had done our chores, of course. I was just hanging around downtown when I was about nine years old and heard the story and got to know this lady. I was fascinated by her grit. To see this very insignificant, socially disenfranchised lady, a single mother, who was willing to march down to the local aristocracy read them the riot act, so to speak, was fascinating."

During the Shelburne interview, Tom further described the woman and her life, "The lady was a really free spirit, modern way beyond the times in my hometown. They got really huffy about her lifestyle. She didn't go to school, but they could get to her through her daughter." The name Harper Valley came from Tom seeing Harpeth Valley Elementary School in Bellevue, Tennessee. He decided to use a similar place name since he liked the sound of the school's name.

"Harper Valley P.T.A" won the 1968 Grammy Award for Best Country & Western Vocal Performance and the CMA Award for Single of the Year. It spent three weeks at number one, sold six million copies, and crossed over onto the pop charts. The song was recorded by a number of female singers from the same time period including Dolly Parton, Norma Jean, Loretta Lynn, and Dotty West. Billy Ray Cyrus included his version of the song on his 1996 album <u>Trail of Tears</u>. Additionally, the song inspired the 1978 comedy film *Harper Valley P.T.A* which led to the T.V. series *Harper Valley P.T.A.* which aired on NBC from January 16, 1981 to August 14, 1982.

The success of "Harper Valley P.T.A." brought attention to Tom's career. His October 1968 release "Ballad of Forty Dollars" became his first top ten hit. The song was inspired by Tom's experiences mowing grass at a cemetery in Olive Hill. He was hired because his aunt was head of the cemetery committee, it was his first job. During funerals, he would shut off his mower and listen to what was happening. In the Shelburne interview, he described his experiences, "The irony is, when somebody else dies, I don't know how it got to be this way, but the rest of the world more or less forgives their sins. They say, 'Oh, he was a wonderful guy, a good person,' which is one of the ironies of philosophy, I think. Then when they were digging the graves, the people digging the graves had a lot of conversations about the economy of dying. You know, 'He's got a brand new pickup. Who's going to get that?' Then it comes down to, the fellow owes me forty bucks, and you're certainly not going to go to the widow and collect it. I guess it's lost."

Tom showed the song "A Week in a County Jail" to producer Kennedy Jackson. Kennedy decided that, due to the unconventional nature of the song with no chorus, the song was unlikely to be picked up by another artist. So, in 1969, Tom released the single "A Week in a County Jail" which became his first number one song. The song was based on Tom's experience of being arrested in Paintsville, Kentucky for driving on expired tags. He was supposed to only spend one night there but it turned into a week since the only judge in the county had to go out of town for a funeral.

In 1972, Tom released his album <u>The Storyteller</u> which included the song "(Old Dogs, Children, and) Watermelon Wine." Tom wrote the song after performing at the Democratic National Convention in Miami Beach, Florida. He went to the hotel bar around 9:30 p.m. and ordered a Canadian blended whiskey, Seagrams 7, and took a seat. There were only two people in the bar, the bartender who was watching Ironside and cleaning glasses and an African American gentleman who was cleaning up.

The man, having very little cleaning to do, asked Tom if he could join him. Tom said yes and the man asked 'How old do you think I am?' The two continued to talk until Tom finished his drink and they said good night. Before heading to his room, Tom wrote down the words "watermelon wine" on a napkin and stuck it in his pocket.

The next morning, Tom was flying to Atlanta, Georgia on his way back to Nashville. While looking for something in his pocket he found the napkin. Since he had nothing to do on the flight, he started looking for something to write on and found the sick bag in the seat pocket in front of him.

He started writing down the experience and how the man had told him that he had turned sixty-eight years old eleven months ago. At the time, Tom didn't know why the man had mentioned that fact but later realized it was probably to explain that he was retired and was either on retirement or social security. Therefore, he was most likely working to fill his spare time or to make extra money.

The next day at his recording session, Tom told Jerry Kennedy about writing the song on the plane. Jerry liked it so Tom cut "(Old Dogs, Children and) Watermelon Wine." The song was recorded about twenty-four hours after it was written.

Tom released his most commercially successful song "I Love" in 1973. The song, which is comprised of only three cords and is two minutes long, reached number one on the country charts. It has been featured in both a Little Debbie and Ford Truck commercial and had been used as the Coors Beers theme song. Tom, during the Shelbourne interview, recalled that he had once heard "I Love" in an elevator and that it was amazing.

After 1986, Tom retired but continued to write songs, sometimes with Miss Dixie, which were recorded by other artists. However, Mercury Records asked him to record a new album while he was spending his winter in Florida. He agreed but asked to record it at Possum Track Studio in the town of Sopchoppy, Florida instead of Nashville. The background vocals were performed by the Dreadful Possum Chorus. The album <u>Songs from Sopchoppy</u> was released in 1996.

Included on the album was the song "Little Bitty," the idea for which originated when Tom was taking a walk in the Australian countryside. He walked past a little white house with a picket fence, a car in front of a wooden garage, and a little dog in the yard. Tom was thinking that it was the great American dream in Australia and "so it's all right to be a little bitty." Tom began writing the song as he continued walking.

After getting back to the hotel, Tom went to the coffee shop and was still thinking about "little bitty" and it being a universal idea. He asked the waitress if "little bitty" meant anything in Australia. She responded yes, that it was something very tiny. Tom thanked her and, according to him, the waitress gave him a look like 'what the hell is this all about.' Tom now knew that "little bitty" meant the same thing in Kentucky as it did everywhere else.

Tom went upstairs to his room, got his guitar, and finished the song all except the last verse. The song was placed in a drawer where it stayed for two years until Tom was preparing to record a demo but didn't have any songs ready. He pulled the song out of the drawer, looked at it, and decided the song should end the way it started. The song goes in a cycle and just starts all over again. Tom wrote the last verse of the song at the bottom of a typed page.

After hearing Tom's recording of "Little Bitty," Alan Jackson decided to record it and release it in 1996. The song reached the number one spot on the country charts.

Tom used to drive through small towns, stopping at little cafes and pool halls so he could look and listen for song ideas. One time, he hitchhiked from Nashville to Chicago, Illinois. There were times when people would ask him if he was Tom T. Hall, he would answer no, that he was Frank Carter. Towards the end of his travels, he was getting recognized more often.

Tom has released several books over the years including the semi-autobiography *Storytellers Nashville* (1979), a novel *The Laughing Man of Woodmont Coves* (1982), *Christmas and the Old House* (1989), and *What a Book!* (1996). His songs have been recorded by multiple artists including Waylon Jennings, George Jones, and Faron Young.

Tom has been the recipient of many awards and honors including an ACM Poet's Awards, a Grammy for the Best Album Notes, and over thirty BMI awards including the Icon award in 2012.

Tom was inducted into the Kentucky Music Hall of Fame in 2002 and the Country Music Hall of Fame in 2008. On June 1, 2014, Tom's song "(Old Dogs, Children and) Watermelon Wine" was ranked number ninety-three on Rolling Stone magazine list of the 100 greatest country songs.

At Tom's home in Tennessee, he has a variety of animals: cats, chickens, peacocks, and wild turkeys. He enjoys growing a vegetable garden and painting.

Isonville, Kentucky

Isonville, Kentucky is an unincorporated community in Elliott County. It's located along Routes 32 and 486 and is east of Sandy Hook. Even though it's unincorporated, the community has a post office that was established in 1866 and was named for an early settler from Virginia, Archibald Ison.

Don Rigsby

Don Rigsby was born February 2, 1968 and was raised in Isonville, Kentucky. He grew up around a family and community of traditional musicians. His great-grandfather was a blind fiddler and his great aunt played guitar and sang mountain songs. Growing up, he attended a Primitive Baptist Church. In an interview with Tony Pence, Don described the experience of singing in church, "Our Baptist faith doesn't call for musical instruments in the church so I learned to sing line singing and doing that from the time I can remember with my hero. Ever since I was big enough to stand in a chair or on a table beside the pulpit, I was singing right next to my dad."

Don observed the experiences that his older brother Ronnie, an accomplished banjo player, had with music. In the Pence interview he described his feelings about Ronnie and his father, "My brother Ronnie was the picker getting the attention in those days and my Dad was so proud of him, and I too wanted my Dad to be proud of me, not realizing until I got older that he was."

At five years old, Don fell in love with an 8-track tape of Ralph Stanley's 1959 recording of "Hill of Home" with Larry Sparks. Don has stated that he learned to sing from that. For his sixth birthday, his parents took him to a Ralph Stanley concert in Ashland, Kentucky so he could hear Ralph sing "Little Maggie." Keith Whitley, who was in Ralph's band at the time and was friends with Don's father, came out in the audience and hoisted Don on his shoulders and took him backstage to meet Ralph.

In a 2006 interview with Craig Shelburne, Don recalled the experience, "I'll never forget that. Ralph was so gracious and kind, and he's always been my friend ever since. He never forgot me! Ralph's nearing eighty years old, and I'm going to be forty in a couple of years, and we're friends from the time I was six. Never did he forget me, never ever, ever. That's pretty profound."

At age twelve, Don started playing guitar and later added the mandolin and fiddle. Don learned about music by attending bluegrass festivals. His interest in music was encouraged by spending time with Keith Whitley and his cousin Ricky Skaggs.

During college at Morehead State University (Morehead, Kentucky), Don pursued a music career. He played music with Charlie Sizemore, a former member of the Ralph Stanley band. After some time, he got a job with Bluegrass Cardinals, then with JD Crowe & the New South, and finally with the Lonesome River Band.

After the Lonesome River Band mostly dissolved, Don remained at Sugar Hill Records where he recorded three solo albums including a gospel album and two albums with guitarist/singer Dudley Connell. He joined the band Longview and, in 1998, they won the IBMA (International Bluegrass Music Association) for "Lonesome Old Home."

In 2001, Don was unsure about whether he wanted to start his own band and had just become a new father so he accepted a position at the Kentucky Center for Traditional Music at Morehead State University. The program was designed to preserve and promote traditional music in all forms.

After eight years, Don left the position to return to music full-time. He decided to start his own band Midnight Call with band members Jesse Wells on fiddle and clawhammer banjo, Robert Maynard on bass, Dale Vanderpool on banjo, and Shayne Bartley on guitar. The album <u>Hillbilly Heartache</u> was released on July 18, 2006 and was his first solo release for Rebel Records. The album featured songs including ones about a moonshining father and an overly confident local hero.

Don has won two SPBGMA Traditional Male Vocalist of the Year awards, a Bluegrass Now Magazine Fan Choice Award for Vocal Tenor of the Year (1999), the 2001 Governor's Kentucky Star Award, and two IBMA awards for his role as producer of Larry Sparks' album <u>40</u> (2005).

Don continues to tour with Midnight Call and is a member of the Band of Ruhks along with his former Lonesome River band mates Ronnie Bowman and Kenny Smith. He is also recording music with David Thom, whom he met through their mutual friend Bill Evans when the three performed at a tribute to Flatt & Scruggs. Don and David hit it off musically and personally, even though they come from different backgrounds. After the tribute concert, David asked Don to California so they could play music together and made plans to record an album together. Their album <u>New Territory</u> was released January 10, 2016.

Don, a married father of two children, still lives in Isonville. He described the joys of living there in the Pence interview, "My kids know their grandparents and go to the church I grew up singing, plus Mom and Dad aren't as young as they used to be, but don't tell Dad."

Sandy Hook, Kentucky

Sandy Hook, located in Elliot County Kentucky, is beside the Little Sandy River and has a population of 675 residents (2010 census). The city was settled in the 1820s and was established by the state legislature in 1850. The name "Sandy Hook" came from the fishhook-shaped bend in the river at the time.

In 1869, Sandy Hook was chosen as the county seat due to a donation of land for public holdings by resident James Hunter. The city was incorporated as Martinsburg, in 1872, as an honor to Rep. John P. Martin. However, the post office was established in 1874 and had to be named "Sandy Hook" since priority was given to another Martinsburg in the state. So, the name "Sandy Hook" was reinstated shortly after and was the town was reincorporated as Sandy Hook in 1888.

Keith Whitley

Jackie Keith Whitley was born in Ashland, Kentucky on July 1, 1955 to Elmer and Faye Whitley. They raised Keith and his older siblings, Dwight, Randy, and Mary, in Sandy Hook, Kentucky. Keith grew up in a musical family, his father played harmonica, his mother played piano, organ, guitar, and banjo, and his grandfather played a five-string banjo.

According to Dwight, Keith could sing as soon as he could speak. His sister Mary stated in an interview with TNN's Life and Times that, "[Keith] came into the world singing." Keith won a local talent contest at four years old. In the Life and Times interview, Faye described the experience, "He won, he sang Marty Robbins "Big Iron," wore a black cowboy outfit. They asked him if he would do another song for us. He just unbuckled his gun belt and let them fall to the floor, threw his hat down, and started singing "I'm a Wandering Soul"." After the contest, the DJ that was emceeing the event suggested that Elmer should buy Keith guitar which he did a week later.

Faye started teaching Keith to play a Stella guitar her sister had made and gave to the family. According to Dwight, the guitar Elmer ordered was from Alden's catalog and cost ten dollars. The case cost either two or three dollars. By the time Keith was seven or eight years old, he was able to play an electric guitar. When Keith was eight years old, his sister Mary wrote a letter to the *Buddy Starcher Show,* which filmed in Charleston, West Virginia, telling them about Keith and asked if he could come in for an interview. The individuals at the program agreed and were so impressed with Keith that he was booked on the show for the following week.

In addition to music, a young Keith enjoyed riding his peddle car up and down the family's driveway. As he got older, he loved to ride motor bikes and motorcycles.

Keith loved music by Lefty Frizzell, George Jones, and Elvis Presley. In the Life and Times interview, Faye recalled how Keith "could just hear [a song] one time and pick it up and start playing it." Dwight, who is eight years older than Keith, had a rock and roll band that Keith joined and became the lead singer of, even though he was the youngest member.

In 1963, Keith became interested in the Stanley Brothers after receiving an album from Dwight, who worked away during the week. Keith's sister-in-law, Flo Whitley, recalls how the interest developed, "[Dwight] listened to Stanley Brothers music, Ralph Stanley, and he brought some of it home to Keith and Keith just kinda latched on to it. And for quite some time, Dwight would bring home a new Stanley Brothers album and by the next weekend, when we came home, Keith would know every song on it."

In an interview promoting his album L.A. to Miami, Keith described his progression from country music to bluegrass, "First off, I've always, all I've ever wanted to be was a country singer but in order to get in a band, you know there were no drummers or electric bass players or steel guitar players in Sandy Hook, Kentucky. So in order to get in a band, that's actually how I got involved in bluegrass music. My brother and some other guys in Sandy Hook had a bluegrass band and I was probably twelve or thirteen at the time when I started playing bluegrass music. So actually what I'm doing now is what I started out doing."

Around 1968, Keith and Dwight had two different local radio shows. One was a live show on WGOH in Grayson, Kentucky. The other was a taped show that aired on WLKX in West Liberty, Kentucky on Saturday and Sunday. The shows were recorded on Wednesday night in the family garage. The Saturday night show consisted of bluegrass music while Sunday night was a combination of bluegrass and gospel. The program was sponsored by Western Auto in Sandy Hook and Mountain Rural Telephone. The shows continued for about five years until Keith began to tour with Ralph Stanley.

Keith met Ricky Skaggs at a talent show when he was fifteen years old. Dwight recalled the evening, "We went to Ezel, Kentucky one night, we couldn't enter the talent contest because we were considered professionals because we were playing on radio. Ricky Skaggs was there with his father and Ricky entered a fiddling contest and so during intermission Keith and Ricky got to talking and they had a lot in common. They both loved the Stanley Brothers and I think there was like six months difference in their ages. Keith invited Ricky to come to perform on our radio show the next week. We taped them on Wednesday night. And my Dad taped them in his garage. Ricky came and brought his father Hobert and so they both played on the next radio show. And so he continued, he became a regular with Keith and with me on our radio show. And that's how that all got started."

Keith and Ricky formed a band, The Lonesome Mountain Boys, and sang mostly Stanley Brothers tunes. The boys had a lot of opportunities to play and quickly became a popular attraction. In 1970, Keith and Ricky met Ralph Stanley at one of his shows. Ralph was running late due to a flat tire so the club owner asked Keith and Ricky if they would be willing to perform. The boys retrieved their instruments from the car and performed Stanley Brothers tunes.

Dwight recalled the events of the evening, "Hobert, Ricky's father, took them to Fort Gay, West Virginia to see Ralph at a place there and Ralph was late, so Ricky and Keith got up there signing and when Ralph came in he heard them and was impressed cause it sounded like a young Ralph and Carter Stanley so he invited them to stay and play on his show. And from there, anytime he would be in the area they would play with him and then when school was out they both went on the road with him full-time."

As a member of Stanley's band The Clinch Mountain Boys, Keith, who played flat-top guitar and sang harmony, recorded seven albums including Crying for the Cross (1971) which was named Bluegrass Album of the Year. In 1973, he left the group and was a member of various bands for the next two years including his own band Country Store and New Tradition that played around Washington D.C.

In 1975, the lead singer of The Clinch Mountain Boys passed away so Ralph asked Keith to rejoin the band as lead singer and front man. Keith agreed and recorded five more albums. During this time, Keith and Ricky also recorded two duet albums. The first was a tribute to the Stanley Brothers and was recorded with a small label in Dayton, Ohio. The second was called Second Generation Bluegrass and featured the boys doing original material and different types of songs.

During this time, Keith met Lester Flatt and the two developed a friendship. In an interview to promote his L.A. to Miami album, he described the relationship, "Well, I got, I had the privilege of getting to know Lester real well. When I was working with Ralph Stanley, we were on the bluegrass circuit together and I spent a lot of time with Lester and got to be real good friends with him. And as a matter of fact, I have a guitar that Lester gave me in 1974 which was a 1943 Herringbone D28 Martin that he had played for years. So I kinda developed an imitation of Lester that he was quite fond of." Keith did the impersonation on his home answering machine and during multiple interviews.

Between 1978 and 1982, Keith was a member of J.D. Crowe & the New South. During this time, he recorded three albums that were a mix of bluegrass and straight country. After leaving Crowe, Keith began to pursue his solo career and ended up signing a record deal with RCA records.

In 1982, Keith moved to Nashville, Tennessee. In 1984, he released his first solo EP (extended play), A Hard Act to Follow, which featured a more mainstream country style. During an interview entitled the Whitley Family Reminisces, Dwight recalled Keith's reaction to the album, "When he brought that tape home, he was so excited about that. He was really into it and wanted us to hear every word." One of the singles on the album, "Turn Me To Love," featured fellow Kentuckian Patty Loveless.

Even though Keith had moved to Nashville to be a singer not a songwriter, he signed a songwriting contract with Tree Publishing in September 1984. However, he didn't actually start writing until the spring of 1985 since he was on a promotional tour. While at Tree, Keith's songs were recorded by various artists. His song "Joseph and Mary's Boy" was included on Alabama's album Alabama Christmas.

In 1986, Keith released his album L.A. to Miami. In an interview promoting the album, Keith said that the album was country, bluegrass, and R&B and was a good example of what he was all about. The album featured the single "Miami, My Amy" which became his first top fifteen song and remained on the charts for twenty weeks. Keith stated that the song blew him away and was his favorite song he had recorded to date. Three other singles featured on the album, "Ten Feet Away," "Homecoming 63," and "Hard Livin," all became top ten hits.

During the recording sessions for his third album, Keith felt that the album sounded the same as its predecessor and that the songs weren't up to the standard he hoped to reach. Keith asked RCA to shelve the fifteen song project and they agreed. Keith expressed an interest in being able to assert more of himself in terms of songs and production. This time, Keith worked with producer Garth Fundis and completed the album Don't Close Your Eyes.

The album was released in 1998 and sold extremely well. It featured three number one singles, "Don't Close Your Eyes," "When You Say Nothing At All," and "I'm No Stranger To The Rain." Billboard Magazine ranked "Don't Close Your Eyes" the number one country song of 1988. Don't Close Your Eyes also included the songs "It's All Coming Back To Me Now" that Keith wrote during his years at Tree Publishing and a remake of Lester Flatt's "I Never Go Around Mirrors" which was a huge hit at concerts.

In early 1989, Keith approached Joe Galante, chairman of Sony Music Nashville, about releasing "I Never Go Around Mirrors" as a single. Even though Galante approved of the musical flexibility Keith had achieved with the song, he suggested something more upbeat. The result was the song "I Wonder Do You Think Of Me," which Keith had previously optioned for another album.

Keith passed away on May 9, 1989 at the age of thirty-three. In addition to his brother, Dwight, and sister, Mary, Keith is survived by his son, Jesse, and a daughter, Morgan.

His fourth studio album, I Wonder Do You Think Of Me, was released on August 1, 1989 and produced two number one hits, the title track and "It Ain't Nothin'."

Following Keith's passing, RCA continued to release albums featuring his work including a Greatest Hits album and Kentucky Bluebird. The album compiled performance clips from his days with the Clinch Mountain Boys, interviews, and previously unreleased material. Included in this was the duet "Brotherly Love" with Earl Thomas Conley which reached number two on the country charts in late 1991.

In September 1994, Keith's friends from bluegrass and country came together to record and release Keith Whitley: A Tribute Album. The album featured covers of Keith's songs by artists including Alan Jackson, Diamond Rio, Alison Krauss and his childhood friend Ricky Skaggs and included previously unreleased tracks Keith had recorded in 1987. Also included was the multi-artist song "A Voice Still Rings True" which featured Sawyer Brown, Ricky Skaggs, John Anderson, Steve Wariner, and Joe Diffie on lead vocals and artists including Mark Collie, T. Graham Brown,

Deborah Allen, Rhonda Vincent, Dean Dillon, Earl Thomas Conley, Larry Cordle, and Tanya Tucker on backing vocals.

Today, Keith, his music, and his extreme talent are still remembered and celebrated by his family, fans, and fellow artists. Stan Hitchcock, former head of CMT, stated that Keith was the "finest young man I believe I ever met." Keith's impact on country music has inspired countless artists. Robert Olberman, musical historian, remarked, "There are artists, young artists, I'm thinking, in particular, Tim McGraw, who can date his interests in becoming a country music singer from hearing "Miami, My Amy" on the radio."

Years ago, the highly talented country artist Kevin Sharp received a request at one of his concerts to sing a Keith Whitley song. He politely declined stating that Keith's talent was so great that he wouldn't attempt to sing one of his songs.

Rising star Mo Pitney, age twenty-three, spoke about Keith Whitley's impact on him musically, "Keith Whitley was one of my biggest heroes and I watched him all the way back to when he was with J.D. Crowe & New South and even as far back as Ralph Stanley. I followed him his whole career; well I went back on videos. I wish I was alive when he was doing all that, I watched videos. He moved on and did his own country thing."

Keith is still fondly remembered in his hometown of Sandy Hook which is evident by a statue of Keith playing his guitar being prominently displayed in a local cemetery. The town has a street named Keith Whitley Boulevard, a display of Keith's belonging at the Laurel Gorge Cultural Center, and a display of photos and event posters at the local Frosty Freeze restaurant.

During an interview with Stan Hitchcock on the program *Heart to Heart*, Keith described going back to Sandy Hook for a benefit concert and the people who had supported him. He remembered the event, "I was in this business, as you know, a long, long time before I ever had a hit record and those people have supported me and believed in me you know like they'd say 'we know it's going to happen someday' you know. And it was really neat last September Labor Day, we got to go back and do a homecoming benefit show for my hometown. The lions club sponsored it and the little gymnasium back there is suppose to seat about eight hundred people and I think we had close to two thousand people crammed in that place and it was just, it was amazing."

Keith's long list of accomplishments includes an ACM Cliffie Stone Pioneer Award, a CMA Award for Single of the Year: "I'm No Stanger To The Rain", a CMA Award for Vocal Event of the Year, and "When You Say Nothing At All" being named the number one country love song of all time. He was inducted into the Kentucky Music Hall of Fame on April 7, 2011.

Kentucky Artists

Kebo Cyrus

Kevin "Kebo" Cyrus is the oldest child of Ron Cyrus and Ruth Ann Adkins. He has three sisters and two brothers, one of whom is fellow performer Billy Ray Cyrus. Kebo grew up in Flatwoods, Kentucky as part of a musical family. On Saturdays, his grandfather, mother, father, and uncle would get together to sing and play bluegrass music. His father was also a part of the gospel group The Crownsmen Quartet, whom performed at revivals and other locations.

At an early age, Kebo learned to play guitar. As kids, him and Billy learned George Jones' songs and would perform them in the family's living room. Additionally, the boys enjoyed being outside where they would climb trees, play hide-n-seek, and build dams.

Kebo attended Russell Independent Schools and graduated from Russell High School (Russell, Kentucky) in 1977. During high school and beyond, he has performed as a member of different bands and as a solo artist. He has traveled a great deal and has performed at a variety of locations including the Grand Ole Opry and the Ryman.

Kebo's most recent album, You Know, features him on lead vocals, guitar, and bass. Today, Kebo, a married father, regularly plays music and sings at his church. He also performs at different venues including raising money for local causes.

A few years ago, he moved back to his childhood home in Flatwoods that he shares with his dogs Sibo and Timber, his cats, a turtle, and a snake. He enjoys being outside with Sibo and Timber where they can enjoy the nature surrounding them.

Kebo hopes to record an album, The Sons of the Crownsmen, with Billy Ray where they would perform the quartet's gospel hits.

Kevin Denney

Kevin Denney was born on January 27, 1978, the only child of Samuel Ray and Elsie Denney. He was raised in Monticello, Kentucky where the family made their living raising cattle and tobacco. His parents, who were one half of a gospel quartet, taught Kevin to enjoy the simple pleasures of life. At age three, they bought him his first guitar. Kevin has been quoted as saying, "I'd sit in front of the TV with that guitar on Saturday nights watching the *Opry* on TV, acting like I was playing around." After his grandmother bought him a banjo at age eleven, Kevin joined his cousin's bluegrass band that performed on the festival circuit.

At age seventeen, Kevin began to consider doing something other than music such as a "real" job. However, his girlfriend at the time took him to a George Strait concert in Lexington, Kentucky for his eighteenth birthday. It was at the concert that he became convinced he wanted a career in music. In an interview with Jeffrey Remz, Kevin described his feelings, "[I] just fell in love with country music. I think it was just the atmosphere. George himself is inspiring. Just the crowd and the lights. It was just what I wanted to do. I wanted to create that for myself."

He continued, "I came back to my hometown and got on the phone and started calling musicians that I knew. I ended up booking a country band together. I booked shows. I did the booking myself. I was eighteen, working with older people than me. I called clubs, festivals." Up until this point, Kevin had only sung bluegrass music.

Kevin moved to Nashville, Tennessee at age twenty to pursue a career in music. In the Remz interview, Kevin remembered the experience, "I wasn't nervous at all. I was just looking forward to going on my own - chasing my goals and dreams. I met up with a lot of songwriters and got to be really good friends with a lot of songwriters. God is good. He put me in the right place." He began working at the apartment complex where he lived and met his eventual producer, Leigh Reynolds, through a mutual friend. Reynolds got him a writing deal and shopped him around.

Kevin signed with Lyric Street Records and released his self-titled debut album in April 2002. The album included several songs Kevin co-wrote and produced three chart-topping hits, "That's Just Jessie," "Cadillac Tears," and "It'll Go Away." Kevin described the style of the album to Remz, "Me and my producer kind of had our own motto before we started - to make music our heroes would be proud of. That's just what we shot for, and I hope we've done it. I would say the two people who influenced my style the most were probably Keith Whitley and George Jones. Just [their] music and personal. I just love the men too. I think those guys are just exceptional. I grew up in the same part of the country that Keith did, so I was influenced by his style."

Kevin continues to write and co-write songs that are recorded by other artists including Craig Morgan's 2009 single "Bonfire," Eastern Corbin's "Don't Ask Me About a Woman" included on his 2010 self-titled debut album, and Dailey & Vincent's "On The Other Side" which won the IBMA (International Bluegrass Music Association) Bluegrass Gospel Song of the Year. He lives in Nashville with his wife, Amber, and their daughter.

John Michael Montgomery

John Michael Montgomery was born January 20, 1965 in Danville, Kentucky to his parents, Harold and Carol Montgomery, who shared a lifelong love of music with their children. John Michael has an older brother, Eddie, who is one half of the duo Montgomery Gentry, and a younger sister, Rebecca.

John Michael's musical influences include Bob Seger, The Eagles, and Lynyrd Skynyrd. He commented on his singing in an interview with Kristen Russell, "I don't hear or see anything special about me singing. I'm not impressed with my voice. Luckily, a lot of people are."

His family's band Harold Montgomery & Kentucky River Express would play on weekends with John Michael and Eddie soaking up the experience. After his parents divorced, John Michael took over as lead singer before forming his own band Early Tymz with Eddie and Troy Gentry. After deciding to pursue a solo career, John Michael was noticed by Nashville talent scouts and got a record deal in the early 1990s.

Throughout his career, John Michael has released multiple albums including his debut album Life's a Dance (1992), John Michael Montgomery (1995), What I Do the Best (1996), Home to You (1999), Pictures (2002), and Letters from Home (2004). In 2008, John formed his own record label, Stringtown Records, and released his album Time Flies. Five of his albums have been certified gold by the Recording Industry Association of America (RIAA). Additionally, his 1994 album Kickin' It Up and his 1995 self-titled album were both certified four times platinum by RIAA.

He has had twenty top ten singles including seven number ones: "I Love the Way You Love Me" (1993), "I Swear" (1993), "Be My Baby Tonight" (1994), "If You've Got Love" (1994), "I Can Love You Like That" (1995), "Sold (The Grundy County Auction Incident)" (1995), and "The Little Girl" (2000). John dedicated his 1996 song "I Miss You A Little" to his father, whom had passed away.

John Michael has been the recipient of many awards and honors including two CMAs (Single of the Year, Horizon Award), three ACMs (New Male Vocalist of the Year, Single Record of the Year,

Song of the Year), and an AMA for Favorite New Country Artist. He was inducted into the Kentucky Music Hall of Fame in 2011.

John Michael is married to his wife, Crystal, and they have a daughter, Madison, and a son, Walker.

Montgomery Gentry

Montgomery Gentry is a duo comprised of Eddie Montgomery and Troy Gentry. Gerald Edward "Eddie" Montgomery was born September 30, 1963 in Danville, Kentucky to his parents Harold and Carol Montgomery. He has two siblings; a sister Rebecca and a brother, fellow performer John Michael. Around age five, Eddie began performing with his parents' band Harold Montgomery & Kentucky River Express. During his teenage years, he became a full-time band member and replaced his mother as the band's drummer.

Troy "T-Roy" Lee Gentry was born April 5, 1967, in Lexington, Kentucky, to his parents Lloyd and Pat Gentry. During his teens, Troy began to do guest vocals with area bands and eventually landed a job with a local group in Lexington.

In 1990, the band Early Tymz was formed with band members including Eddie, Troy, and John Michael. After the band broke up, the trio performed as Young Country. John Michael served as lead vocalist until he decided to pursue a solo career and everyone went their separate ways. In 1994, Troy won the Jim Beam National Talent Search in Nashville, Tennessee which led to him opening for various artists including John Michael and Tracy Byrd.

After Troy was unable to find a record deal as a solo artist, he reunited with Eddie and the two formed the duo Deuce. They performed at local nightclubs and later changed their name to Montgomery Gentry. In 1999, the duo signed with Columbia Records.

Since signing their record deal, they have continued to record and release albums including their debut Tattoos & Scars (1999), Back When I Knew It All (2008), and Folks Like Us (2015). The Recording Association of America (RIAA) has certified three of their albums gold: Carrying On (2001), Something to Be Proud Of: The Best of 1999–2005 (2005), and Some People Change (2006) and three of them platinum: Tattoos & Scars (1999), My Town (2002), and You Do Your Thing (2004).

Montgomery Gentry has had sixteen top ten hits including five number one singles: "If You Ever Stop Loving Me" (2004), "Something to Be Proud Of" (2005), "Lucky Man" (2007), "Back When I Knew It All" (2008), and "Roll with Me" (2008). The duo has also won numerous awards including eleven CMAs, ten ACMs, an AMA, and a Grammy Award for Best Country Vocal Performance by a Duo or Group: "Lucky Man" in 2008. In 2015, Montgomery Gentry was inducted into the Kentucky Music Hall of Fame.

Today, Troy is married to his wife, Angie, and has two daughters. He enjoys spending time at the gym and with his family. Eddie, a father and avid University of Kentucky sports fan, still lives in Kentucky.

Dwight Whitley

Dwight Whitley, the son of Elmer and Faye Whitley, was raised in Sandy Hook, Kentucky. He has one sister and two brothers, one of whom is artist Keith Whitley. Dwight grew up listening to his grandfather play the banjo and, by the age of ten, was able to play himself. He also learned to play the guitar and harmonica. In high school, he played in a rock and roll band, The Ramblers. He made the switch to bluegrass and formed the band the Whitley Brothers with Keith.

Dwight dedicated his album Brotherly Love to his brothers, Keith and Randy, both of whom had passed away. Included on the album was the single "The Legend and the Man." The video for the song told part of Keith's story and featured Dwight's son, John, playing Keith. In 2000, Dwight released his follow-up album Nothin' But A Woman.

Dwight, a car and Harley Davidson motorcycle enthusiast, still lives in Sandy Hook with his wife, Flo, and is a father and grandfather.

Chris Stapleton

Christopher "Chris" Alvin Stapleton was born on April 15, 1978 in Lexington, Kentucky and grew up in Staffordsville, Kentucky. Chris, the son of a coal miner, has an older brother and younger sister. He graduated from Johnson Central High School (Paintsville, Kentucky) and briefly attended Vanderbilt University (Nashville, Tennessee).

In 2001, Chris decided to pursue a music career and signed a songwriting publishing deal with Sea Gayle Music. Over one hundred of Chris's songs have been recorded by various artists including George Strait, Luke Bryan, Kenny Chesney, Darius Rucker, Dierks Bentley, Thomas Rhett, and Josh Turner. He has also co-wrote songs for artists such as Vince Gill and Peter Frampton.

During the 2016 ASCAP Awards, Chris remarked, "When I found out you could have a job being a songwriter, I thought, 'Man, that's the greatest job in the world. I gotta figure how to do it'." He also gave a "shout out" to fellow award winner Ricky Skaggs and recalled how he once tried to get him to sign his mandolin.

From 2008-2010, Chris joined the band The SteelDrivers as their lead singer and guitarist. During this time period, The SteelDrivers won the International Bluegrass Music Association (IBMA) Emerging Artist of the Year award. After leaving The SteelDrivers, Chris formed the band The Jompson Brothers who performed Southern rock.

In 2013, Chris signed a record deal with Mercury Nashville as a solo artist. He released his debut album, <u>Traveller</u>, in 2015. Chris's wife, Morgane, helped him sort through fifteen years of songs to determine which nine he would record. The album was inspired by a road trip Chris and Morgane took after his father passed away in 2013.

Chris has won multiple awards and honors including two 2016 Grammy Awards (Best Country Album: <u>Traveller</u> and Best Country Solo Performance), five CMAs (Album of the Year-2015, Male Vocalist of the Year-2015 and 2016, New Artist of the Year-2015, and Music Video of the Year: "Fire Away"-2016), three 2016 ACMs (Album of the Year: <u>Traveller</u>, Song of the Year: "Nobody to Blame," and Male Vocalist of the Year), and the 2016 ASCAP Vanguard Award.

At the 2016 CMA Awards, Chris performed the Willie Nelson and Ray Charles duet "Seven Spanish Angels" with Dwight Yoakam. Upon receiving his Male Vocalist award, Chris remarked, "It means so much to get to be a part of country music, these are the best people in the world."

He lives in Nashville with Morgane, a fellow songwriter, and their two children.

Tommy Webb Band

Tommy Webb is from Langley, Kentucky and started singing and playing guitar around age fifteen. He didn't grow up in a musical family but his great grandfather played the fiddle. Tommy's musical influences include the Stanley Brothers, Flatt & Scruggs, Merle Haggard, and Ricky Skaggs. Charlie Hall, of WCYO-FM in Richmond Kentucky, described Tommy as "the real deal...being from Eastern Kentucky, he lives and breathes bluegrass music."

While in high school, Tommy and his friends played music together. Around age twenty, Tommy started performing with different bands including The Pine Top Ramblers, South Creek, and Southern Bluegrass Boys. In 2005, he formed the Tommy Webb Band where he sings lead tenor. Tommy plays guitar and the clawhammer banjo on occasion.

The Tommy Webb Band has released multiple albums including Heartland, Eastern Kentucky, and Rock-N-Roll to Bill Monroe. As a songwriter, Tommy has written several songs featured on the band's albums such as "Eastern Kentucky," "Now That You Are Gone," and "If It Weren't For Bluegrass Music (I'd Go Crazy)."

The other members of the band are from various locations and backgrounds. Jamie Shannon is from Louisa, Kentucky and joined the band in 2012. He started playing music at age ten and can play the mandolin, guitar, bass, and banjo. Chad Gilbert, the newest member, is from Grayson, Kentucky and plays bass in the band.

Jim Burchett learned to play banjo at eight years old and, by the age of fifteen, was playing throughout Eastern Kentucky with his friends Keith Whitley and Ricky Skaggs. He joined the Tommy Webb Band in 2013 and plays banjo and sings harmony. Additionally, he is able to play guitar, mandolin, and bass. Dave

Webb is from Langley, Kentucky and has been the band's road manager for ten years.

Tommy describes one of his greatest experiences with the band being when they traveled to Finland to play a festival.

Author's note: The following artist, Kevin Sharp, is not from Kentucky but due to his remarkable talent, long list of charitable contributions, and his kind and giving personality, he has earned the right to be included in this book (and any other for that matter). Kevin overcame overwhelming obstacles and setbacks that would have derailed so many to become a performer. By doing so, he shared his amazing voice, his love, and the positive way he lived his life with so many people.

Kevin Sharp

Kevin Grant Sharp was born on December 10, 1970 in Redding, California to his parents Glen and Elaine Sharp. He grew up in a musical home with his five older brothers, three sisters, and numerous foster siblings.

Glen, a bishop in church, owned a legal company that provided multiple services to lawyers and the court system. Elaine, a retired schoolteacher, wanted the family to have dinner together, attend church on Sundays, and for her children to do the right thing.

The family lived in a small country house in Cottonwood, California where they raised chickens, pigs, sheep, goats, a cow, and a bull. The older boys slept in bunk beds on the back porch. Kevin and his brothers enjoyed catching frogs when the backfields would flood. All of the kids had daily chores and, after receiving their allowance on Saturday, the older siblings would take the younger ones to the store for candy.

Glen loved music and had dreamed of having a music career when he was younger. As a child, Kevin took piano lessons and tried his hand at various other instruments but never stuck with any of them. He started performing with his family at church when he was three years old. At around four or five years of age, he started performing musical shows for his family by standing on the coffee table and singing or lip syncing John Denver, Barry Manilow, and Glen Campbell songs. He would make up tickets to sale but usually ended up giving them away for free.

In 1979, Glen was putting in long hours at his company and that, combined with worry, caused his health to start to fail. As a result, he sold his business and the family moved to Weiser, Idaho. Glen purchased and ran a quiet little restaurant in the small town of about 4,000 residents.

Kevin mowed lawns for spending money and his father would give free ice cream to him and his friends. He played sports throughout junior high and high school except for his eighth grade year when he suffered a leg injury. In high school, Kevin enjoyed working out with weights, was in the school choir, and performed at churches with his family.

The business that his father had sold in California began to fail and the new owner was about to lose everything including the money he owed Glen. With few options available, the family moved back to California after eight years in Idaho.

Kevin began his sophomore year at Bella Vista High School in Fair Oaks, California. Life there was a culture shock after living in Idaho for so long. Everything felt backward to Kevin except football.

In the summer of 1987, Kevin began to experience knee and back pain which caused him to limp. After a doctor's visit, it was determined that he must have suffered a sports injury that was slow to heal. Due to the pain, he didn't feel well enough to play football or basketball his senior year.

As the pain continued, Kevin began to lose his physical strength which caused him to let go of his dream of playing college football. Despite his declining health, doctors continued to say that it was a prolonged sports injury. Kevin had to use crutches at his senior prom and limped through graduation.

After graduation, Kevin auditioned for Music Circus, a summer stock group that gives amateurs the opportunity to work with professional actors and singers that are between paying jobs. After getting the job, he thought that this experience may be what he needed to put his illness behind him so that he could start college in the fall. Unfortunately, the work was difficult and he collapsed on stage. As a result, the director had to let him go.

Kevin's pain had become unbearable, he would lay awake for days unable to eat, sleep, or think. After another trip to the emergency room, he was sent home in the middle of the night with prescription pain relievers to help him get some sleep. The following morning, Kevin's girlfriend came to visit and found him in his room unable to breathe. Paramedics returned him to the emergency room he had left a few hours before.

This trip to the hospital was different from the previous ones. He was admitted to the hospital for x-rays, blood work, and an MRI. Two doctors delivered the news to Kevin, age eighteen, that he had Ewing's Sarcoma, a type of bone cancer. In addition to the tumor in Kevin's leg, he also had a spot on one of his lungs.

Since the cancer was so advanced and there were no proven drugs, it was suggested that Kevin return home and spend his last few months with his family. The following day, Kevin's oncologist came to his room and asked if he wanted to try an experimental treatment. Kevin, feeling that he had nothing to lose, immediately agreed.

He was transported to the hospital daily since he was receiving both radiation and chemotherapy treatments. His family came to be by his side and support him.

Four months into his treatments, a Make-A-Wish representative visited Kevin and asked him what he would wish for. He decided he would like to meet music producer David Foster. Kevin, his parents, and his younger sister, Genni, flew to Los Angeles, California and visited David's studio where they watched him work. In his autobiography *Tragedy's Gift*, Kevin described the experience, "The Make-A-Wish Foundation had a huge impact on my survival. The strength and blessing I received that day truly helped to save my life."

About eight months after his diagnosis, some of Kevin's friends started coming by and watching TV or playing video games with him. Kevin's physical appearance had changed dramatically since he had lost a large amount of weight and his hair. In a show of solidarity, one of his friends shaved his head so that Kevin wouldn't feel out of place.

Nearly a year into his treatments, Kevin reluctantly convinced two of his friends to take him out driving around. After stopping by the side of the road, Kevin decided to climb on top of a brick wall to see what was on the other side. The result was a broken leg and surgery to have to the bone repaired with a metal rod that would aid in the healing process.

During surgery, the doctor performed a procedure to check and see if the treatments were working. The tumor on his lungs looked better but his leg looked the same. The radiation therapy hadn't shrunk the tumor but it had managed to weaken his bone which is why it broke when he fell.

In *Tragedy's Gift*, Kevin recalled his reaction, "This news caused a huge, enormous setback for me. I was clinging by a thread to any hope of living and now I was being told that all my intense suffering, pain, and ravage to my family were to no avail. How could this be? What were my options? I was not ready to die."

The following days were filled with phone calls, research, and medical inquires on Kevin's behalf. His doctor presented him with one last option, a form of chemotherapy that would bring him as close to death as a person can get without actually dying. The treatment would take a year and make the past year seems easy. There were discussions about his hospital stays being longer, potential side effects, and intense pain as the cancer was being fought off. In the end, Kevin decided to do the treatment and prayed that he would survive.

One night during one of his many stays in the hospital, Kevin, who was extremely ill and groggy from pain, experienced a life-altering event. He felt a presence in the room urging him to give up his fight and die. He was paralyzed with fear but eventually managed to squeak out a yelp that awoke his father. Kevin told him 'He's trying to get me.' When his father asked who, he answered the Devil. The feeling happened two more times, each becoming more intense. The third time, Kevin asked his father to pray which helped to ease his fear. After his father returned to bed, Kevin had another visitor but this time it brought pure peace. He felt no pain, no fear. He wasn't sure if the visit was from an angel or God himself but he was assured that cancer was not his destiny.

Kevin's second round of treatments were so horrible that he thought he wouldn't survive. He would sometimes lose his ability to fight but visualizing himself as a successful singer helped keep him sane. He would picture himself performing, singing to fans, or on his tour bus writing songs. In addition to his daydreams, Kevin would visit the other pediatric rooms and sing for the kids and their families. He would perform "Please Don't Be Scared" by Barry Manilow and other songs that had helped him through difficult times.

After his second year of treatments, Kevin received the news that his cancer was in remission. This caught him off guard and he was unsure how to move forward. He was still experiencing pain and nausea. His doctors had assured him that his hair would grow back but instead it came back in thin and patchy. So, with his self-confidence at an all-time low, he made the decision to shave his head. He immediately felt better since he was used to being bald and now he was a guy that decided to shave his head.

After a rough period of dealing with the psychological and physical side effects of his illness and treatments, Kevin decided to pursue his dream of a music career. He knew that he needed to have his own songs and, therefore, needed a co-writer. He paired up with his brother Richard's college friend, Eric Bunch, who dreamed of being a famous songwriter. The two immediately hit it off and decided to move forward.

Kevin enrolled in music and recording classes at the local community college. His father and Richard helped him to build SharpSounds studio in the family garage. After the construction, soundproofing, and equipment installation was complete, Eric flew from Utah to California so that Kevin could record a demo. They worked five days straight with little sleep to complete the project so Kevin could shop for a deal.

Kevin was proud of the finished product and sent it everywhere. While he waited for a deal, he took a job singing at funerals, joined a local band, and sang at a theme park in Northern California.

After receiving a phone call from someone in David Foster's office, Kevin had the opportunity to fly to Los Angeles to meet with Chris Fannin and to audition for Kyle Lehning with Asylum Records. When he performed his songs, he pretended he was on stage in front of thousands of fans. He gave it everything he had and pretended he was the biggest thing in the music industry. After the audition, Lehning came up, shook his hand, and said 'Let's do this.'

Kevin wanted every song included on his first album to be one he loved and could see himself singing hundreds of times. He wanted to have memories of his time in the studio so he asked all of the musicians for their autographs. Once the album was complete, Kevin hit the road to promote it.

Kevin's album, <u>Measure of a Man</u>, was released on September 24, 1996, was certified gold, and reached number four on the country charts. His first single, "Noboby Knows," spent four weeks at number one on the Billboard Hot Country Single &Tracks chart. Kevin's follow-up singles "She's Sure Taking It Well" and "If You Love Somebody" were top ten hits.

In a 1997 article in Country Weekly, Kevin recalled the first time he heard himself on the radio, "I was in Kentucky, headed to a radio function, just driving along and it caught me completely off guard. It was one of the most amazing experiences of my life. I just started screaming and yelling and everybody in the car thought I was nuts and was about to cause an accident. I was so numb, it was like an out-of-body experience."

After Kevin's visit with David Foster, he wrote a letter of gratitude to the Sacramento Chapter of Make-A-Wish where he vowed to always be a wish kid and to help the foundation whenever he could. Seven years later, he received a phone call from his manager saying that a seven year old boy loved the song "Nobody Knows" and wished to meet the person who sang it. Kevin flew to Houston, Texas to meet Matthew who was extremely ill and had little time left. Matthew was unable to speak and barley conscious but smiled briefly when Kevin sang "Nobody Knows." The experience was overwhelming but it allowed him to fulfill his promise. More importantly, Kevin was able to give love and encouragement to a child who was fighting to stay alive and to help a family through a devastating time.

Over the years, Kevin continued to work with the Make-A-Wish Foundation. He become a national spokesman for the organization and granted the wish of many children. Kevin extended an open invitation to patients in every town in which he had tour stops.

Kevin performed the song "If You Believe" on the *Annabelle's Wish* soundtrack released in 1997. *Annabelle's Wish* is an animated Christmas movie that focuses on the friendship between Annabelle, a young calf, who aspires to fly and become one of Santa's reindeer and Billy, a young boy, who is mute. A portion of the sales of the movie benefited the Make-A-Wish Foundation. The following year, Kevin rode on the *Annabelle's Wish* float in the Macy's Thanksgiving Day Parade.

Kevin's second album Love Is was released on June 23, 1998 on the Elektra/Asylum label. That same year, he did an interview with Wendy Newcomer promoting the album and his single "Love Is All That Really Matters." During the interview, he discussed his upbringing, "I've always been raised to believe that loving one another and treating one another as you'd want to be treated was the most important thing. Everything else kind of takes care of itself when you do that. This song is true to the way my parents raised me."

In 2004, Kevin released his autobiography *Tragedy's Gift* which he wrote with Jeanne Gere. The book included details about his childhood, cancer battle, and how he got his start in country music. On July 26, 2005, Kevin released his album Make A Wish on Cupit Records. The songs featured on the album included the "Your Love Reaches Me," "I Think I'll Stay," and "Make a Wish."

Kevin passed away on April 19, 2014 in Fair Oaks, California due to complications arising from past stomach surgeries and digestive issues that were the result of his past treatments. His music and inspiring life are remembered and celebrated by Kevin's family, fellow musicians, and fans. Artist John Berry remarked, "Kevin was such a great talent and a wonderful guy. His passion for all that is important in life was an inspiration."

Artist Jimmy Fortune remembered all the work Kevin had done with Make-A-Wish and other charities, "He fought for so many causes. To feel his spirit was a blessing for me. That was his first and foremost thing, how could he help other people? It was a blessing to get to know him and see what he was all about. He was put here for a reason, he brought us some great music and singing, but he also brought us a great sense of strength for us to carry on through the hard times."

Wayne Warner, whom had recorded with Kevin, described him as an amazing soul and said, "He was just a joy to work with. If he wasn't feeling well, you wouldn't know it. He was such a gentle soul, and had such a giving heart."

Country musician Ty Herndon remembered and celebrated Kevin by saying, "I shared the stage many times with Kevin Sharp. He was such a fantastic person and such a great singer. Journey on my brother and sing with the Angels. Love you brother."

Throughout his career, Kevin received many awards and honors including the CMA New Touring Artist of the Year Award, being named the Make-A-Wish Foundation's Celebrity Wish Granter of the Year, CMTs Rising Male Video Star of the Year Award, and the Gilda's Club (Gilda Radner Foundation) It's Always Something Award (for a life that teaches and inspires).

"Billy Ray Cyrus." *Wikipedia: The Free Encyclopedia.* Wikimedia Foundation, Inc. 22 July 2004. Web. 25 Oct. 2105.
Biography.com Editors. "Billy Ray Cyrus Biography." *The Biography.com Website.* A&E Networks Television. Web. 25 Oct. 2015.
"Billy Ray Cyrus Biography." *BIOGRAPHY: Billy Ray Cyrus.* Lifetime. Web. 25 Oct. 2015.
"Billy Ray Cyrus, Kellie Pickler Cast in New CMT Comedies." CMT.com. Web. 25 Oct. 2015.
"Billy Ray Cyrus Biography." *Luck Media Marketing Inc.* LuckMediacom. Web. 25 Oct. 2015.
Davidson, Gregg. "Billy Ray Cyrus Series." The Greenup Beacon. Web. 30 Oct. 2015.
Vinson, Christina. "Watch the First Promo for Billy Ray Cyrus' 'Still the King'" *The Boot.* Taste of Country Network. 23 Mar. 2016. Web. 28 Mar. 2016.
Beck, Glenn. "Billy Ray Cyrus Interview." *CNN.* Cable News Network, 27 Jan. 2007. Web. 15 Nov. 2015.
Cyrus, Kevin "Kebo". Personal interview. Oct. 2015.
"The Judds." *Wikipedia: The Free Encyclopedia.* Wikimedia Foundation, Inc. 22 July 2004. Web. 14 Oct. 2015.
"The Judds Discography." Wikipedia*: The Free Encyclopedia.* Wikimedia Foundation, Inc. 22 July 2004. Web. 14 Oct. 2015.
"Naomi Judd." *Wikipedia: The Free Encyclopedia.* Wikimedia Foundation, Inc. 22 July 2004. Web. 15 Oct. 2015.
"Wynonna Judd." *Wikipedia: The Free Encyclopedia.* Wikimedia Foundation, Inc. 22 July 2004. Web. 14 Oct. 2015.
"Wynonna Judd Discography." *Wikipedia: The Free Encyclopedia.* Wikimedia Foundation, Inc. 22 July 2004. Web. 14 Oct. 2015.
"The Judds Interview with Greta van Susteren - 10.16.10." *YouTube.* YouTube, 26 Oct. 2010. Web. 13 Oct. 2015.
"Come Some Rainy Day." *Wikipedia: The Free Encyclopedia.* Wikimedia Foundation, Inc. 22 July 2004. Web. 11 Nov. 2016.
"Come Some Rainy Day (Live W/ Ashley Judd) - Wynonna Judd." *YouTube.* YouTube, 8 Feb. 2015. Web. 13 Nov. 2016.
Puente, Maria. "The Judds to Reunite in Vegas." *USA Today.* Gannett, 2015. Web. 16 Oct. 2015.
Messer, Lesley. "Naomi Judd Discusses Her Relationship With Daughters Wynonna and Ashley." *ABC News.* ABC News Network. Web. 16 Oct. 2015.
Juett, James. "Judd History Long and Local." The Daily Independent. Web. 16 Oct. 2015.
"Wynonna." *Contemporary Musicians.* Encyclopedia.com. 2005. Web. 19 Mar. 2016
"Wynonna & the Big Noise" on the Way in February." *WWGP 1050 AM Mainstream.* ABC News. Web. 09 Nov. 2105.
"Boyd County's Wynonna & Naomi Judd." Country Music Highway. Web. 11 Nov. 2015.
"Welcome to Ashland, KY." Ashland, KY. Web. 30 Nov. 2015.
"Winona, Arizona." *Wikipedia: The Free Encyclopedia.* Wikimedia Foundation, Inc. 22 July 2004. Web. 30 Nov. 2015.
"Patty Loveless." *Wikipedia: The Free Encyclopedia.* Wikimedia Foundation, Inc. 22 July 2004. Web. 04 Oct. 2015.
"Patty Loveless." Patty Loveless. Web. 28 Oct. 2015.
"Patty Loveless." Grand Ole Opry. 2013. Web. 28 Oct. 2015.
"Patty Loveless Bio." CMT Artists. Web. 04 Oct. 2015.
Lye, Bethany. "At Home with Patty Loveless: Away from It All." People. 2008. Web. 28 Oct. 2015.
Roland, Tom. "Georgia On Her Mind." Country Weekly. 30 Apr. 2002: 42-43. Print.

"Loretta Lynn." Billboard Magazine. Web. 17 Oct. 2015.
"Loretta Lynn." *Wikipedia: The Free Encyclopedia.* Wikimedia Foundation, Inc. 22 July 2004. Web. 17 Oct. 2015.
"Loretta Lynn Discography." *Wikipedia: The Free Encyclopedia.* Wikimedia Foundation, Inc. 22 July 2004. Web. 17 Oct. 2015.
"Loretta Lynn." *Biography.* A&E Networks Television. Web. 17 Oct. 2015.
"Loretta Lynn's Full Life." NPR. 8 Nov. 2010. Web. 04 Nov. 2015.
"Gary Chapman Interviews Loretta." *Prime Time Country.* YouTube. Web. 04 Nov. 2015.
"About Loretta Lynn: Still a Mountain Girl." *American Masters.* PBS. Web. 04 Nov. 2015.
"Loretta Lynn Awards." *IMDb.* IMDb. Web. 04 Jan. 2015.
Betts, Stephen. "Crystal Gayle Reflects on 'Slick Country' and Coal Miner's Family." *Rolling Stone.* Rolling Stone. 22 Sept. 2014. Web. 18 Oct. 2015.
"Crystal Gayle." *Wikipedia: The Free Encyclopedia.* Wikimedia Foundation, Inc. 22 July 2004. Web. 18 Oct. 2015.
Maness, Jessi. "Crystal Gayle Talks Fame and Family." *Sports and Entertainment Nashville.* Sports and Entertainment Nashville, 03 Nov. 2014. Web. 11 Nov. 2015.
Dauphin, Chuck. "Crystal Gayle Says Country Hall of Fame Exhibit Gives Her a Chance to 'Look Back'" Billboard. 09 Sept. 2014. Web. 18 Oct. 2015.
James, Gary. "Crystal Gayle Interview." *Crystal Gayle Interview.* Gary James, Web. 08 Nov. 2016.
"Crystal Gayle - Country Music Career." *CMT.* YouTube. Web. 06 Nov. 2015.
"Crystal Gayle Interview." Country Stars Central. Web. 04 Nov. 2015.
"Crystal Gayle Interview and Performance." Thunder Valley Casino Resort Interview. YouTube. Web. 06 Nov. 2015.
"Crystal Gayle- 4 Webbs." *Pop! Goes the Country. YouTube.* YouTube. Web. 06 Nov. 2015.
"True Love (Crystal Gayle Album)." *Wikipedia: The Free Encyclopedia.* Wikimedia Foundation, Inc. 22 July 2004. Web. 12 Nov. 2016
"Clara Webb Butcher, Loretta Lynn, Crystal Gayle Final." *YouTube.* YouTube. Web. 06 Nov. 2015.
"Brown, Frank "Hylo" (1922-2003)." Miami University Hamilton. Web. 15 Oct. 2015.
"Frank "Hylo" Brown 1922-2003." RootsWeb: KYKNOTT-L [KYKNOTT] Obituary. Web. 15 Oct. 2015.
"Hylo Brown- Bluegrass singer with a wide vocal range." The Independent. 06 April 2003. Web. 15 Oct. 2015.
"Johnson County's Hylo Brown." Country Music Highway. Web. 01 Oct. 2015.
Ankeny, Jason. "Hylo Brown" AllMusic. Web. 06 Oct. 2015.
Brown, William Timothy. Personal interview. Sept. 2015.
Boyd, Tommy. Personal interview. Sept. 2015.
Purk, Bill. Personal interview. Sept. 2015.
Alexander, Floyd. Personal interview. Sept. 2015.
" Gary Stewart 'Lost talent' of country music whose hits included 'She's Actin' Single (I'm Drinkin' Doubles)'."The Independent. 19 Dec. 2003. Web. 29 Oct. 2015.
"Gary Stewart." *Wikipedia: The Free Encyclopedia.* Wikimedia Foundation, Inc. 22 July 2004. Web. 29 Oct. 2015.
"Gary Stewart "Let's Go Jukein" on Nashville Now." *YouTube.* YouTube. Web. 06 Nov. 2015.
"Tennessee Woman." *Wikipedia: The Free Encyclopedia.* Wikimedia Foundation, Inc. 22 July 2004. Web. 07 Nov. 2015.
"Jenkins Homecoming Festival Days- 1998." The Fress Press. 11 May 1998. Web. 02 Feb. 2016.
"Smoking in the Rockies." Sawyer Brown Wiki. Web. 07 Nov. 2015.

"The way we were- Clips from Mountain Eagle front pages over the past 50 years." *The Mountain Eagle*. The Mountain Eagle. 13 Aug. 2008. Web. 06 Feb. 2016.
Stewart, Shannon. Personal interview. Dec. 2015.
Lewis, Mike. Personal interview. Dec. 2015.
Greer, Lois. Personal interview. Oct. 2016.
Hill, Lorena. Personal interview. Oct. 2016.
Flint, Ernestine. Personal interview. Oct. 2016.
"Gary Stewart: Harlan County Highway Lyrics." LyricWikia. Web. 29 Nov. 2015.
"Country Music Highway- Gary Stewart." *Letcher County Community News-Press.* Letcher County Community News-Press. 9 Sept. 1998. Web. 06 Feb. 2016.
Dennis, Paul. "Country Heritage: Gary Stewart – A Short Life Of Trouble (1944-2003)." My Kind of Country. 16 May 2011. Web. 01 Nov. 2015.
Shelburne, Craig. "In the Words of Tom T. Hall ..." CMT. 03 Aug. 2005. Web. 26 Oct. 2015.
"About Tom T. Hall." CMT Artists. Web. 22 Oct. 2015.
Cooper, Peter. "Tom T. Hall: How the Storyteller Found His Voice." *MusicWorld*. BMI.com. 18 May 2012. Web. 28 Oct. 2015.
Hall, Tom T. "61: Old Dogs, Children and Watermelon Wine." 61: Old Dogs, Children and Watermelon Wine. Chicken Soup for the Soul. Web. 28 Oct. 2015.
Conaway, Alanna. "Tom T. Hall Talks Retirement and Living the Simple Life." Nash Country Weekly. 01 June 2014. Web. 14 Oct. 2015.
"Unusual Kentucky: Tom T. Hall." Unusual Kentucky: Tom T. Hall. 05 Jan. 2011. Web. 28 Oct. 2015.
Pacella, Megan. "No. 71: Tom T. Hall, 'Old Dogs, Children and Watermelon Wine' – Top 100 Country Songs." Taste of Country. Web. 11 Nov. 2015.
Levin, Al. "Tom T. Hall." Sun Sentinal. 09 Mar. 1997. Web. 16 Oct. 2015.
Hurst, Jack. "Tom T. Hall (1936 –)." Encyclopedia of Appalachia. 01 Mar. 2011. Web. 20 Oct. 2015.
The Boot Staff. "Story Behind the Song: Jeannie C. Riley, 'Harper Valley PTA'" *The Boot*. Taste of Country Network, 5 Feb. 2016. Web. 23 Apr. 2016.
"Harper Valley P.T.A." *Wikipedia: The Free Encyclopedia*. Wikimedia Foundation, Inc. 22 July 2004. Web. 23 Nov. 2015.
"Harper Valley P.T.A. (film)." *Wikipedia: The Free Encyclopedia*. Wikimedia Foundation, Inc. 22 July 2004. Web. 23 Nov. 2015.
"Harper Valley P.T.A. (TV series)." *Wikipedia: The Free Encyclopedia*. Wikimedia Foundation, Inc. 22 July 2004. Web. 23 Nov. 2015.
"Trail of Tears (Billy Ray Cyrus album)." *Wikipedia: The Free Encyclopedia*. Wikimedia Foundation, Inc. 22 July 2004. Web. 23 Nov. 2015.
"Billy Ray Cyrus/ Harper Valley PTA" *YouTube*. YouTube, 8 Nov. 2008. Web. 23 Nov. 2016.
"Keith Whitley Bio." CMT Artists. Web. 06 Oct. 2015.
"Keith Whitley Biography." *IMDb*. IMDb. Web. 04 Nov. 2015.
"Keith Whitley." *Wikipedia: The Free Encyclopedia*. Wikimedia Foundation, Inc. 22 July 2004. Web. 04 Oct. 2015.
"Keith Whitley: A Tribute Album." *Wikipedia: The Free Encyclopedia*. Wikimedia Foundation, Inc. 22 July 2004. Web. 06 Oct. 2015.
"The Life and Times of Keith Whitley." *TNN*. YouTube. Web. 04 Nov. 2015.
"Keith Whitley & Stan Hitchcock." YouTube. Web. 04 Nov. 2015.
"Keith Whitley and Ralph Emery." *Nashville Now*. *YouTube*. YouTube. Web. 04 Nov. 2015.
"The Whitley Family Reminisces (Pt. 1 of 5)." *YouTube*. YouTube, 8 Nov. 2008. Web. 20 Nov. 2016.

"The Whitley Family Reminisces (Pt. 2 of 5)." *YouTube.* YouTube, 8 Nov. 2008. Web. 20 Nov. 2016.
"Country Songs Year End 1988." *Billboard.* Billboard, Web. 3 Dec. 2016.
Whitley, Dwight. Personal interview. Dec. 2015.
Whitley, Flo. Personal interview. Dec. 2015.
"Keith Whitley, Death, 1989, Stan Hitchcock Speaking." *YouTube.* YouTube. Web. 06 Nov. 2015.
"Dwight Yoakam Biography." *IMDb.* IMDb. Web. 28 Oct. 2015.
"Dwight Yoakam." *Wikipedia: The Free Encyclopedia.* Wikimedia Foundation, Inc. 22 July 2004. Web. 28 Oct. 2015.
"Singer-songwriter Dwight Yoakam." *Travis Smiley Interview.* PBS. Web. 01 Nov. 2015.
Lundy, Ronni. "Shuck Beans, Stack Cakes, and Honest Fried Chicken." *Google Books.* Atlantic Monthly Press, 01 July 1994. Web. 03 Nov. 2015.
"Buenas Noches from a Lonely Room." *Wikipedia: The Free Encyclopedia.* Wikimedia Foundation, Inc. 22 July 2004. Web. 02 Nov. 2015.
"Guitars, Cadillacs, Etc., Etc.." *Wikipedia: The Free Encyclopedia.* Wikimedia Foundation, Inc. 22 July 2004. Web. 02 Nov. 2015.
"3 Pears." *Wikipedia: The Free Encyclopedia.* Wikimedia Foundation, Inc. 22 July 2004. Web. 02 Nov. 2015.
"Dwight Yoakam albums discography." *Wikipedia: The Free Encyclopedia.* Wikimedia Foundation, Inc. 22 July 2004. Web. 02 Nov. 2015.
"Dwight Yoakam's "Swimmin' Pools, Movie Stars..." *Sugar Hill Records.* Concord Music Group, 2 Aug. 2106. Web. 24 Oct. 2016.
"Dwight Yoakam Plots Bluegrass Album - Rolling Stone." *Rolling Stone.* Rolling Stone, 8 Aug. 2016. Web. 24 Oct. 2016.
"I Sang Dixie." *Wikipedia: The Free Encyclopedia.* Wikimedia Foundation, Inc. 22 July 2004. Web. 02 Nov. 2015.
"Dwight Yoakam - I Sang Dixie" *YouTube.* You Tube, 13 June 2011. Web. 24 Oct. 2016.
"Dwight Yoakam Miner's Prayer." *YouTube.* YouTube. 24 Feb. 2008. Web. 22 Apr. 2016.
"Dwight Yoakam Induction Speech." *YouTube.* YouTube. 24 Feb. 2008. Web. 22 Apr. 2016.
Meredith, Kyle. "Catching Up With Dwight Yoakam." *Paste Magazine.* Paste Media Group, 4 Sept. 2014. Web. 08 Nov. 2015.
Skaggs, Garold. Personal interview. Oct. 2015
Skaggs, Janie. Personal interview. Oct. 2015.
"Ricky Skaggs." *Bio.* A&E Networks Television. Web. 05 Oct. 2015.
"The Story." Ricky Skaggs. Web. 05 Oct. 2015.
"Ricky Skaggs: "Kentucky Traveler: My Life in Music" - The Diane Rehm Show." The Diane Rehm Show. 15 Aug. 2013. Web. 04 Nov. 2015.
Skaggs, Ricky. "Read From Ricky Skaggs' Memoir, Kentucky Traveler." *CMT News.* Viacom, 16 Aug. 2013. Web. 20 Nov. 2015.
"Ricky Skaggs." *Wikipedia: The Free Encyclopedia.* Wikimedia Foundation, Inc. 22 July 2004. Web. 04 Oct. 2015.
"Fiddle | Jason Carter." Jason Carter. Web. 21 Mar. 2016.
"Jason Carter." All Music. Web. 21 Mar. 2016
Preston, Tim. "Music for the Road: Fiddler Jason Carter Joins Legendary Names along Country Music Highway." The Independent. 17 June 2015. Web. 21 Mar. 2016.
"Del McCoury Band" The Kurland Agency. Nov. 2011. Web. 21 Mar. 2016.
Hauenstein, George. "Jason Carter: That On the Move." Country Standard Time. 1997. Web. 21 Mar. 2016.
"About." The Travelin' McCourys. Web. 21 Mar. 2016.

Williams, Portia. "Carter Added to Country Music Highway." Portsmouth Daily Times. 17 June 2015. Web. 16 Apr. 2016.
"Recipient History." *IBMA.* International Bluegrass Music Association, Web. 07 Nov. 2016.
"About." *Del McCoury Band.* The Del McCoury Band 2016. Web. 07 Nov. 2016.
Preston, Tim. "Jason Carter." *The Daily Independent.* The Daily Independent, 24 Jan. 2014. Web. 7 Nov. 2016.
Osborne, Mike. "90 Second Spin: Michael Cleveland Releases "Fiddler's Dream"" *WMOT.* WMOT, 3 Nov. 2016. Web. 7 Nov. 2016.
"Sundy Best." *Wikipedia: The Free Encyclopedia.* Wikimedia Foundation, Inc. 22 July 2004. Web. 21 Mar. 2016. 2015.
Copley, Rich. "The Best Seems Yet to Come for Kentucky Duo Sundy Best." *LexGo.* Herald Dispatch. 01 Mar. 2014. Web. 22 Mar. 2016.
Gibson, Jordan M. "Nick Jamerson." *Alumni Spotlight.* University of Pikeville. 21 May 2013. Web. 22 Mar. 2016.
Parton, Chris. "Sundy Best Make an Impression With Moving." CMT Edge. 26 Aug. 2013. Web. 22 Mar. 2016.
"Sundy Best." Wortman Works. Web. 22 Mar. 2016.
Wheat, Jack. "Monumental Weekend for Kentucky Favorite Duo Sundy Best." Wortman Works. 16 Feb. 2015. Web. 22 Mar. 2016.
Hudak, Joseph. "Watch Sundy Best Hit the Drive-In in Retro 'Four Door' Video." *Rolling Stone.* Rolling Stone. 01 July 2015. Web. 09 Apr. 2016.
Stephens, Samantha. "Sundy Best - Exclusive Interview CMT Listen Up." *CMT.* YouTube. 06 Apr. 2016. Web. 09 Apr. 2016.
Petty, Mark. "Hear sits down with Sundy Best." *HEAR.* HEAR Magazine. 21 Mar. 2014. Web. 09 Apr. 2016.
Irr, Tim. "WSAZ First Look at Four Sundy Best Benefit Concert Interview." *WSAZ.* YouTube. 23 July 2015. Web. 09 Apr. 2016.
Harris, Preshias. "The New Dynamic Duo: Sundy Best - Music News Nashville." Music News Nashville. 12 Mar. 2014. Web. 09 Apr. 2016.
Philpott, Amber. "A Conversation with Ky. Duo, Sundy Best." WKYT. 26 Aug. 2013. Web. 09 Apr. 2016.
"Don Rigsby." All Music. Web. 23 Mar. 2016
Shelbourne, Craig. "Don Rigsby Heeds the Bluegrass Call." CMT News. 11 Aug. 2006. Web. 23 Mar. 2016.
"Rebel Records Recording Artist Don Rigsby." Rebel Records. Web. 23 Mar. 2016.
"Don Rigsby." Don Rigsby and David Thom. Web. 23 Mar. 2016.
Kaufman, Steve. "Don Rigsby." Flatpik Central. Web. 23 Mar. 2016.
Pence, Tony. "Don Rigsby's 'High Lonesome Sound' Makes This Music Man Worth A Listen." Tony Pence RSS. 2013. Web. 29 Mar. 2016.
Carter, Liv. "Songwriters Circle: Josh Osborne." *Urban Country News.* Black River Publishing, 14 Apr. 2013. Web. 16 Oct. 2016.
Diamond, Rick. Josh Osborne and Toni Osborne Photos. 25 Mar. 2014. *Getty Images North America.* Zimbio. Web. 12 Oct. 2016.
"Josh Osborne." SMACKSONGS. Web. 12 Oct. 2016.
"Josh Osborne." *Wikipedia: The Free Encyclopedia.* Wikimedia Foundation, Inc. 22 July 2004. Web. 10 Oct. 2016.
"Merry Go 'Round (Kasey Musgraves Song)." *Wikipedia: The Free Encyclopedia.* Wikimedia Foundation, Inc. 22 July 2004. Web. 1 Dec. 2016.
Conger, Bill. "Josh Osborne Co-Writes #1 Hits for Sam Hunt, Blake Shelton, Keith Urban And Other Artists." Songwriter Universe Songwriting News Articles Song Contest. 23 Nov. 2015. Web. 14 Sept. 2016.

Matthew Cramer. "GRAMMY-WINNING SONGWRITER JOSH OSBORNE ADDED TO US 23 COUNTRY MUSIC HIGHWAY IN PIKE COUNTY." *Black River Publishing.* Black River Entertainment, 13 June 2014. Web. 14 Sept. 2016.
"Josh Osborne." Country Music Highway. Web. 14 Sept. 2106.
Copley, Rich. "Songwriter from Kentucky Will Be at Grammys to See If He's a Winner." *LexGo.* Herald Leader, 25 Jan. 2014. Web. 14 Sept. 2016.
"Molly O'Day." *Wikipedia: The Free Encyclopedia.* Wikimedia Foundation, Inc. 22 July 2004. Web. 23 Oct. 2016.
"Molly O'Day." *Kentucky's US 23 Country Music Highway.* Country Music Highway, 2014. Web. 15 Oct. 2016.
Neace, James Clell. "Country Music's "Molly O'Day"" Kentucky Explorer. 2000. Web. 24 Oct. 2016.
"Molly O'Day | Biography." *ALLMUSIC.* RhythmOne Group, Web. 18 Oct. 2016.
"Molly O'Day." *Discogs.* Discogs, Web. 24 Oct. 2016.
Rockwell, John. "MOLLY O'DAY, SINGER OF COUNTRY MUSIC IN ROUGHHEWN STYLE" *The New York Times.* The New York Times, 8 Dec. 1987. Web. 18 Oct. 2016.
Sanders, Ked. "Mountain Santa Claus Coming to Letcher County." *Letcher County Community News Press.* Letcher County Community News Press. 2 Dec. 2009. Web. 25 Oct. 2016.
"Marlow Tackett Top Songs." Music VF. Web. 25 Oct. 2016.
"Marlow Tackett." *Discogs.* Discogs, Web. 25 Oct. 2016.
Contract Construction. 1982. Billboard. Web.
Sanders, Ked, and Patsy Tackett. "Marlow Tackett Will Headline Jenkins Homecoming Days Festival." *The Mountain Eagle.* The Mountain Eagle, 8 Aug. 2008. Web. 21 Oct. 2016.
"Marlow Tackett Obituary." *Hall and Jones Funeral Home.* Hall and Jones Funeral Home, May 2014. Web. 22 Oct. 2016.
United States. Kentucky Senate. *15 RS BR 1807.* 16 Dec. 2015. Web. 6 Oct. 2016.
Friend, Racheal. Personal interview. Oct. 2016.
"Group Honored on Country Music Highway." *Williamson Daily News.* Heartland Publications, 17 Jan. 2010. Web. 28 Nov. 2016.
"Country Western group honored with signs on Country Music Highway." *Williamson Daily News.* Heartland Publications, 11 Jan. 2010. Web. 28 Nov. 2016.
Legislature doc- 08 RS HJR 24
"Montgomery Gentry." Montgomery Gentry. Web. 01 Dec. 2015.
"Montgomery Gentry Biography." *IMDb.* IMDb. Web. 01 Dec. 2015.
"Montgomery Gentry." *Wikipedia: The Free Encyclopedia.* Wikimedia Foundation, Inc. 22 July 2004. Web. 01 Dec. 2015.
"Montgomery Gentry discography." *Wikipedia: The Free Encyclopedia.* Wikimedia Foundation, Inc. 22 July 2004. Web. 01 Dec. 2015.
"About." John Michael Montgomery. Web. 01 Dec. 2015.
"John Michael Montgomery Biography." *IMDb.* IMDb. Web. 01 Dec. 2015.
"John Michael Montgomery." *Wikipedia: The Free Encyclopedia.* Wikimedia Foundation, Inc. 22 July 2004. Web. 01 Dec. 2015.
"John Michael Montgomery discography." *Wikipedia: The Free Encyclopedia.* Wikimedia Foundation, Inc. 22 July 2004. Web. 01 Dec. 2015.
Russell, Kristen. "John Michael Montgomery." Country Weekly 18 Apr. 2000: 38-39. Print.
"Kevin Denney." Cowboy Christian Connection. Web. 01 Dec. 2015.
Remz, Jeffrey B. "Kevin Denney Goes Strait for Country." Country Standard Time. May 2002. Web. 01 Dec. 2015.
Monte, William Lynwood. "Grassroots Music in the Upper Cumberland." Google Books. Web. 01 Dec. 2015.

"Kevin Denney." *Wikipedia: The Free Encyclopedia*. Wikimedia Foundation, Inc. 22 July 2004. Web. 01 Dec. 2015.
"Dwight Whitley Fan Page." DWFP. Web. 02 Dec. 2015.
"Dwight Whitley News!" Mi2N. 23 Apr. 2000. Web. 24 Apr. 2016.
"Bio." Larry Cordle. Web. 02 Dec. 2015.
"About Larry Cordle & Lonesome Standard Time." *CMT Artists*. CMT, Web. 26 Oct. 2016.
"Larry Cordle." *Wikipedia: The Free Encyclopedia*. Wikimedia Foundation, Inc. 22 July 2004. Web. 02 Dec. 2015.
"Murder on Music Row." *Wikipedia: The Free Encyclopedia*. Wikimedia Foundation, Inc. 22 July 2004. Web. 20 Oct. 2016.
"Larry Cordle Discography." *ALLMUSIC*. ALLMUSIC, Web. 28 Oct. 2016.
Netherland, Tom. "Larry Cordle Is Country by Place, in Spirit and in Song." *SWVa Today*. SWVa Today, 4 Feb. 2010. Web. 28 Oct. 2016.
"Larry Cordle." *U*.S. 23 COUNTRY MUSIC HIGHWAY Travel Guide 2010: 23-24. Web.
"GEORGE STRAIT LYRICS - Murder On Music Row." *azlyrics*. musixmatch, Web. 28 Oct. 2016.
"About." Chris Stapleton. Web. 04 Dec. 2015.
"Chris Stapleton." *Wikipedia: The Free Encyclopedia*. Wikimedia Foundation, Inc. 22 July 2004. Web. 01 Dec. 2015.
Leahey, Andrew. "See Chris Stapleton Cover Willie Nelson, Ray Charles at CMA Awards." *Rolling Stone*. Rolling Stone, 2 Nov. 2016. Web. 6 Nov. 2016.
Houghton, Cillea. "Chris Stapleton Claims New Male Vocalist of the Year at the 2016 CMA Awards." *Taste of Country*. Taste of Country Network, 3 Nov. 2016. Web. 6 Nov. 2016.
"Kevin Sharp." AirPlay Direct. 16 Oct. 2014. Web. 05 Apr. 2016.
Sharp, Kevin, and Jeanne Gere. Tragedy's Gift. Cincinnati, OH: ZassCo, Inc Pub., 2004. Print.
Dauphin, Chuck. "Kevin Sharp Remembered By Fellow Country Artists Wayne Warner, Jimmy Fortune." Billboard. 24 Apr. 2014. Web. 04 Apr. 2016.
"Anabelle's Wish Soundtracks." *IMDb*. IMDb. Web. 07 Apr. 2016.
Newcomer, Wendy. *Country Weekly* 18 Apr. 2000: 60. Print.
Mansfield, Brian. "Fellow Country Singers Remember Kevin Sharp." *USA Today*. Gannett, 22 Apr. 2014. Web. 09 Apr. 2016.
"Kevin Sharp." *Wikipedia: The Free Encyclopedia*. Wikimedia Foundation, Inc. 22 July 2004. Web. 06 Apr. 2016.
"Anabelle's Wish." *Wikipedia: The Free Encyclopedia*. Wikimedia Foundation, Inc. 22 July 2004. Web. 07 Apr. 2016.
Alsup, Dave, and Todd Leopold. "Country Singer Kevin Sharp Dies." *CNN*. CNN. 21 Apr. 2014. Web. 10 Apr. 2016.
Grippo, Robert M., and Christopher Hoskins. Macy's Thanksgiving Day Parade. Charleston, SC: Arcadia, 2004. Print.
"About." Country Music Highway. Web. 13 Oct. 2015.
Taylor, Chuck. "Asylum's Kevin Sharp Proves A Natural Working Country's Promotional Front Line." *Google Books*. Billboard, 4 Oct. 1997. Web. 24 Nov. 2016.
"Kentucky's Contribution for American Music..." Kentucky Music Hall of Fame. Web. 13 Oct. 2015.
"Flatwoods." *Wikipedia: The Free Encyclopedia*. Wikimedia Foundation, Inc. 22 July 2004. Web. 30 Oct. 2015.
"Ashland." *Wikipedia: The Free Encyclopedia*. Wikimedia Foundation, Inc. 22 July 2004. Web. 30 Oct. 2015.
"Pikeville." *Wikipedia: The Free Encyclopedia*. Wikimedia Foundation, Inc. 22 July 2004. Web. 30 Oct. 2015.

"Van Lear." *Wikipedia: The Free Encyclopedia.* Wikimedia Foundation, Inc. 22 July 2004. Web. 30 Oct. 2015.
"River." *Wikipedia: The Free Encyclopedia.* Wikimedia Foundation, Inc. 22 July 2004. Web. 30 Oct. 2015.
"Jenkins." *Wikipedia: The Free Encyclopedia.* Wikimedia Foundation, Inc. 22 July 2004. Web. 30 Oct. 2015.
"Olive Hill." *Wikipedia: The Free Encyclopedia.* Wikimedia Foundation, Inc. 22 July 2004. Web. 30 Oct. 2015.
"Sandy Hook." *Wikipedia: The Free Encyclopedia.* Wikimedia Foundation, Inc. 22 July 2004. Web. 30 Oct. 2015.
"Betsy Layne." *Wikipedia: The Free Encyclopedia.* Wikimedia Foundation, Inc. 22 July 2004. Web. 30 Oct. 2015.
"Betsy Layne, KY." Unusual Kentucky. Web. 13 Nov. 2016.
"Isonville." *Wikipedia: The Free Encyclopedia.* Wikimedia Foundation, Inc. 22 July 2004. Web. 23 Mar. 2016.
"Lloyd." *Wikipedia: The Free Encyclopedia.* Wikimedia Foundation, Inc. 22 July 2004. Web. 23 Mar. 2016.
"Prestonsburg." *Wikipedia: The Free Encyclopedia.* Wikimedia Foundation, Inc. 22 July 2004. Web. 23 Mar. 2016.
"Cordell." *Wikipedia: The Free Encyclopedia.* Wikimedia Foundation, Inc. 22 July 2004. Web. 28 Oct. 2016.
"McCarr." *Wikipedia: The Free Encyclopedia.* Wikimedia Foundation, Inc. 22 July 2004. Web. 6 Nov. 2016.
"McVeigh." *Wikipedia: The Free Encyclopedia.* Wikimedia Foundation, Inc. 22 July 2004. Web. 6 Nov. 2016.
"Virgie." *Wikipedia: The Free Encyclopedia.* Wikimedia Foundation, Inc. 22 July 2004. Web. 9 Nov. 2016.
"Dorton." *Wikipedia: The Free Encyclopedia.* Wikimedia Foundation, Inc. 22 July 2004. Web. 6 Nov. 2016.
"McCarr, KY Profile: Facts, Map, & Data." *KY HomeTownLocator.* HTL, Web. 9 Nov. 2016.
"East Kentucky Science Center." *Wikipedia: The Free Encyclopedia.* Wikimedia Foundation, Inc. 22 July 2004. Web. 23 Mar. 2016.
"Hatfield-McCoy feud." *Wikipedia: The Free Encyclopedia.* Wikimedia Foundation, Inc. 22 July 2004. Web. 28 Mar. 2016.
"Population Estimates, July 1, 2015, (V2015)." Kentucky QuickFacts from the US Census Bureau" Web. 30 Oct. 2015.
Highlands Museum and Discovery Center. Country Music Highway exhibit. Ashland, Kentucky.

Made in the USA
Middletown, DE
09 July 2024